"From the pen of a veteran Reformed pastor comes this hugely helpful compendium of practical Christian wisdom to lead beli... ing their weight in a local church. It is the l I have yet seen. Like the Bible, this book sh consulted often; not only by Baptists, but w is the congregation's goal. Some volumes me down-to-earth publication is one of them."

Dr. James I. Packer
Professor, conference speaker and author of many volumes, including
Knowing God and *Evangelism and the Sovereignty of God*

"As soon as I saw the return address on the package, I expected that I was in for a treat—and I wasn't disappointed! I plunged into it and read it through in a day. I'm speaking about Curtis Thomas' new book, *Life in the Body of Christ*. It was all I expected, and more. Here is a volume that you will want to hand to every member of your church—whether new or old. In his usual style, Curtis combines solid biblical teaching with easy-to-read, practical instructions about issues vital to every member of a congregation. This book fills a niche not previously dealt with. I cannot commend it highly enough."

Dr. Jay E. Adams
Retired Seminary Professor and Pastor, author of over 100 volumes, including *Competent to Counsel* and *Shepherding God's Flock*

"Biblical, spiritual, practical and sensible, this book fills a gaping hole in contemporary Christian literature. Curtis Thomas pours into these pages over forty years of fruitful experience in local church life and witness. They deserve to be widely read and will surely be of outstanding help to all who do so with a willingness to learn."

Dr. John Blanchard
Worldwide conference speaker, author of many volumes including
Right with God, Whatever Happened to Hell? and *Does God Believe in Atheists?*

"*Life in the Body of Christ* is a practical and comprehensive handbook that should prove useful to every layperson in the local church. To my knowledge, there is nothing like it in print that addresses so many issues in such down-to-earth fashion. Even difficult subjects so often encountered in the church are faced head-on in a loving but insightful manner."

Jerry Bridges
Author of a number of books, including *The Pursuit of Holiness* and *Trusting God*

"Life in the Body of Christ is yet another much-needed book from Curtis Thomas packed with theological soundness, pastoral wisdom and practical guidance. Every church member should read it and use it regularly. How many problems in churches could be solved quickly if the wise advice contained in this volume were conscientiously followed by church members."

> **Joel R. Beeke**
> Professor, Puritan Reformed Theological Seminary, Pastor, Heritage Netherlands Reformed Congregation, author of many books, including *A Quest for Full Assurance* and *A Reader's Guide to Reformed Literature*

"A lot is said today about 'dysfunctional' families. Any group of sinful people who live together in close proximity for very long are going to experience some level of dysfunction! What my friend Curtis Thomas has done for us in this book is to provide practical help for minimizing our dysfunction in the family of God. My hope is that this text can press all of us toward unity in the body of Christ. And a pastor would be wise to present this book as a gift to new members who join their church."

> **Bob Lepine**
> Co-Host, FamilyLife Today, frequent speaker, FamilyLife Marriage Conferences, author of *The Christian Husband*

"Life in the Body of Christ is a must read for every Christian. Every age group in every evangelical church should make it a point to study this book chapter by chapter, look seriously at every suggestion, and meditate on every Scripture suggested for that purpose. Curtis Thomas has given us a gift, a stimulus to edifying reflection and action on every pertinent aspect of corporate and individual responsibility and privilege to be pursued in the life of a local church. His suggestions are brief but turgid with biblical insight and healthy church experience. His questions are provocative of the most Christ-honoring train of thought. The variety of subjects that he introduces prompts a real seriousness about the comprehensiveness of Christian worship, discipleship, fellowship and witness. Don't miss this simple but mature guide to an ever-increasing conformity to Christ-centered, Bible-warranted church life."

> **Dr. Thomas J. Nettles**
> Professor of Historical Theology, The Southern Baptist Theological Seminary, author of more than a dozen books, including *By His Grace and for His Glory*

"Curtis Thomas has a heart to see believers enjoy *Life in the Body of Christ* as God intended it to be. Drawing on his years of pastoral ministry, he provides practical wisdom concerning the privileges and responsibilities of being a part of a local congregation of believers. His counsel, if followed, would undoubtedly avert much potential confusion and conflict in local churches, and would certainly bring blessing to the people of God and glory to Christ, the Head of the church."

> **Nancy Leigh DeMoss**
> Host of "Revive our Hearts" radio ministry and author of several works including *A Place of Quiet Rest* and *Lies Women Believe*

"This eminently practical work from the pen of Curtis Thomas will prove helpful to a broad array of constituencies for years to come. For example, it would greatly benefit new believers as they assimilate into Bible-believing local churches. It would also serve well as a text for new members' classes along with those surveying the fundamentals of the faith. Its bite-sized and well-written articles will be found appealing to all."

> **Dr. George Zemek**
> Director, The Ministry Training Center at The Bible Church of Little Rock, AR, author of *Doing God's Business God's Way* and *A Biblical Theology of the Doctrines of Sovereign Grace*

"When I first saw the title of this book by Curtis Thomas, *Life in the Body of Christ*, I thought it might be a duplication of a book I coauthored called *Life in the Father's House*. However, as I read through the book I became aware that his book actually was a companion volume to our book in that it covered many very helpful and practical issues with which our book does not deal. In my opinion, this book will provide in succinct form much useful information on a large variety of everyday issues that ordinary church members face. I encourage people to purchase the book, read it, study it and follow the many practical directives that are found in it. By so doing the individual Christian and the church corporate will be strengthened and blessed."

> **Dr. Wayne Mack**
> Past Chairman, Biblical Counseling Department, The Master's Seminary, copastor, Grace Fellowship Church of the Lehigh Valley author of several volumes, including *Down, But Not Out*

"I am very enthusiastic about *Life in the Body of Christ*. It is a very well organized survey of the manysided privileges and responsibilities of Christian church members. Each chapter includes a basic presentation, often with a set of questions by which a person may evaluate his/her performance in this area. Then there are listed points of application for individuals and for groups. A brief passage of Scripture for meditation concludes the chapter. Any church should benefit by the dissemination and study of this work, especially those that accept Baptist Ecclesiology. I plan to use this book to test my own faithfulness as a church member from time to time.

I don't agree with the author's understanding of restrictive passages about women's ministry, but the list of activities that he views as open to women shows a concern for making sure that the church should reap the benefits of spiritual gifts that God gave to our sisters, who thus would have an opportunity to exercise them."

> **Dr. Roger Nicole**
> Visiting Professor of Theology, Reformed Theological Seminary,
> Orlando, author and conference speaker

"Curtis Thomas has condensed decades of church ministry into a few dozen, easy-to-understand pages. *Life in the Body of Christ* is versatile enough to work as a text in a new Christian's class to ground spiritual babes in the Christian life, in a new member's class, or in a small group study to help believers at all levels of maturity grow as part of Christ's church."

> **Donald W. Whitney**
> Seminary Professor, author of several volumes, including *Spiritual Disciplines for the Christian Life* and *Spiritual Disciplines Within the Church*

"Being a member of a church and serving within the body of Christ is not to be taken lightly. As a result, Curtis Thomas has written an excellent volume to practically help Christians function biblically along with others in the church. The book is easy to read, full of Scripture, challenging in its application and very appropriate for individual or group study. I highly recommend *Life in the Body of Christ*."

> **Martha Peace**
> Biblical counselor and author of *The Excellent Wife* and *Attitudes of a Transformed Heart*

"What does it mean to be a church member? Curtis Thomas has provided us an excellent compendium designed to instruct church members in the practice of living together in the body of Christ. This primer will help leaders upgrade the interest and involvement of members, new or old. We are again indebted to this veteran author and Christian leader for providing practical tools for our work."

Jim Elliff
Christian Communicators Worldwide, Pastor, conference speaker and author, *Pursuing God: A Seeker's Guide*

"I believe that *Life in the Body of Christ: Privileges and Responsibilities in the Local Church* by Curtis Thomas, will prove to be a very useful text for members of the body of Christ. It is a simple and practical expression of how Christians can be better and more effective in their churches and in their lives."

Dr. D. James Kennedy
Senior Minister, Coral Ridge Presbyterian Church, Chancellor, Knox Theological Seminary, President, Evangelism Explosion International

"*Life in the Body of Christ* is a much needed tool to further equip church members to be vital and growing parts of the body of Christ. Curtis Thomas not only describes the most common issues faced by church members and leaders, but provides helpful insights and practical counsel to address them for the glory of Christ and for the sake of church unity. Though some may find views presented to differ from their own churches' confessional standards in a few matters of secondary importance, the general principles and sound biblical counsel articulated by Pastor Thomas are of great benefit to every believer who is concerned about biblical truth and being a faithful member of Christ's church."

Tim J. Reed
Sr. Pastor, Covenant Presbyterian Church, Little Rock, AR

"It has been my privilege over the years to use Curtis' material, and he has done it again with an excellent manual on life in the Church. He covers many of the areas we all wrestle with from spiritual leadership in the family to very practical areas of church ministries and problems. I highly recommend it."

Dr. Frank M. Barker, Jr.
Pastor Emeritus, Briarwood Presbyterian Church, Birmingham, AL

"Curtis Thomas has penned a marvelously instructive book on daily life in the body of Christ. I don't know of another book on the Christian's relationship to the Church that is quite like it. With brief yet thoroughly written chapters on virtually every aspect of church life, this resource is destined to become a practical standard for how to relate to our Lord and His blood-bought saints within a local assembly. Whether you are a pastor, elder, deacon, or in some other function of church leadership, you will find forty-plus years of skilled counsel which has come out of Thomas' own applied knowledge of Scripture and deep local church ministry experience. Equally, whether you are a layman with a long and fruitful ministry in the local church, or a new believer in Jesus who knows very little about your relationship to fellow believers, this book has been written with you in mind. Having been his colleague in pastoral ministry for several years, I can confidently say that Curtis Thomas knows of what he writes in these pages. I pray that this unique volume would become widely read and thoughtfully applied. Follow his guidance and you will enjoy life in the body of Christ!"

> **Dr. S. Lance Quinn**
> Pastor-Teacher, The Bible Church of Little Rock, AR, coauthor, *The Five Points of Calvinism: Defined, Defended, Documented*

"In our day the church is no longer the object of appreciation, devotion and commitment. Curtis Thomas has provided for all of us, in general, and leaders, in particular, an excellent teaching tool for discipleship, as well as, a primer for believers to properly engage in the church to the fullest blessing that God intended and the fullest devotion to which He calls us. The body of Christ, His glorious bride, was purchased by His blood and is headed into eternity."

> **Dr. Harry P. Reeder**
> Sr. Pastor, Briarwood Presbyterian Church, Birmingham, Al, conference speaker, author, *From Embers to a Flame*

"Curtis Thomas loves the Church! And his unique book *Life in the Body of Christ* celebrates his love by providing encyclopedic wisdom for living out the glorious mystery of the Church. Individuals and families will turn to this book again and again for winsome biblical advice."

> **R. Kent Hughes**
> Pastor, College Church, Wheaton, Illinois, author of *Disciplines of a Godly Man*

"Today's Christians have largely lost sight of what it means to be a member of a local congregation. In far too many cases, the local church has been turned into a voluntary association, and church membership has been reduced to a matter of occasional participation and minimal involvement. Curtis C. Thomas knows that the Bible calls us to a far higher vision. Now retired after almost a half-century in ministry, Thomas writes with a wealth of experience that he draws from deep wells of conviction. These short chapters will instruct, encourage and inform. *Life in the Body of Christ* offers a wealth of wisdom and points the way towards a recovery of biblical church membership."

> **Dr. R. Albert Mohler, Jr., President**
> Joseph Emerson Brown Professor of Christian Theology
> The Southern Baptist Theological Seminary, Louisville, KY

"This book is a compendium of wisdom about a neglected topic—churchmanship. Curtis Thomas writes as one who has been seasoned by a life consumed with the study of the Word of God, with years of pastoral experience and the godly maturity of a gracious saint who has run the race and kept the faith. His insights into the nature of the Christian life, the needs of God's people and the centrality of the church in the plan of God are superlative. This is a great book. If widely read and taken to heart, it will revitalize God's people and strengthen Christ's church."

> **Dr. Tedd Tripp**
> Sr. Pastor, Grace Fellowship Church, Hazelton, PA, conference speaker, author of *Shepherding a Child's Heart* and *Hints for Parents: With Gospel Encouragements*

"My first introduction to Curtis Thomas was through his immensely helpful book on the five points of Calvinism. What I still like best about that book is the way it outlines the subject with plain simplicity and precision. It instantly clears away a lot of the cobwebs of confusion for people who are struggling to understand a complex issue. *Life in the Body of Christ* has the same kind of straight-to-the-point clarity. It's a wonderful overview of what church life ought to be. I think it will be a valuable resource—not only for people who are new to the church, but also for seasoned pastors and church leaders looking for a simple roadmap in an age when church ministry has begun to seem unnecessarily complex."

> **Phillip R. Johnson**
> Executive Director, Grace to You radio ministry, author and conference speaker

Life in the Body of Christ

Privileges and Responsibilities
In the Local Church

Curtis C. Thomas

 Founders Press

Committed to historic Baptist principles
Cape Coral, Florida

Published by

Founders Press

Committed to historic Baptist principles

P.O. Box 150931 • Cape Coral, FL 33915
Phone (239) 772-1400 • Fax: (239) 772-1140
Electronic Mail: founders@founders.org or
Website: http://www.founders.org
©2006 Founders Press

Printed in the United States of America

ISBN: 0-9713361–8–0

Throughout this material the titles "pastor," "elder," "shepherd," "minister," "bishop" and "overseer" may be used synonymously. The Scriptures use these titles for the same office and work (see 1 Timothy 3:1–7, 4:6; 5:17–20; Titus 1:5–9; 1 Peter 5:1–4 and Acts 20:28), so they will be used here interchangeably.

If you find portions of this material helpful and wish to use them for the benefit of others, please feel free to do so. We only ask that the publisher be contacted first when excerpts exceed 500 words.

Dedication

This book is dedicated to the pastors/elders, deacons, staff and members of The Bible Church of Little Rock, a rich fellowship of people who take the Word of God as their rule of faith and practice. While not perfect, this body of believers and her leaders strive to live out the many biblical principles mentioned in this book. It is a joy and a gracious gift of God that my wife and I have the privilege of being a part of this congregation.

and to

Tom Arnold, Wade Arnold, Don Bailey, Rob Bailey, David Booth, Charles Borth, Jim Brown, George Cain, Keith Danforth, Rich Daniel, Jimmy DeMoss, Larry Fisher, Richard Fulenwider, Ted Gibson, B. W. Hendricks, Theron Howard, Gary Huitink, Carl Hunt, Tim McCoy, Frank McFerrin, Brian Olmstead, Ben Rush, Jerry Samons, Bill Simmons, Tom Strickland, Lawrence Stolzer, Bill Thomas, Dr. Jack Somers, Kevin Sontag, Calvin Squires, Jim Viner, Joe Walker, Henry Wood, Olin Wright and to the men in our Wednesday morning Bible study and prayer time.

Men, your commitment to Christ and your many years of friendship, prayers, fellowship, support, encouragement and help in so many ways have been a constant source of blessings to me, my family and my ministry.

Introduction

Several years ago my book, *Practical Wisdom for Pastors*, was completed. After forty four years in the ministry I wanted to leave something in print for new pastors coming on the scene which might benefit them as they face everyday practical issues.

Having also been a church member for almost sixty years, it occurred to me that there is not, to my knowledge, a work in print which addresses a large variety of everyday issues which ordinary church members regularly face. There are many books that deal very adequately with *some* of these areas. At the end of this work I have provided a brief list of those resources. It is not an exhaustive bibliography. In fact, there is such a large number of books on the subject that, should I have tried to list them all, you might have found it discouraging to dig through the list. But I believe that you will find the ones included to be helpful.

The work you hold in your hand is designed to discuss a number of subjects, but in less detail, than some of the books included in the list of resources mentioned above. To give them a thorough treatment would have taken the book beyond its purpose. Rather it is hoped that the work will be suggestive and will provide practical ways in which members can better serve their congregations and, ultimately, be better servants of our Lord. To help facilitate that, these discussions are designed to be interactive. At the end of each article there are questions to answer and specific suggestions for you to implement, both individually and in a group setting.

The Word of God teaches us that our Lord gave His life for His church, that He loves His church and that He gave gifts to His church to use in His Kingdom until He returns to take her to glory. His church here on earth is not perfect, but Christ assures us that the gates of hell shall not prevail against it. Samuel J. Stone captures this theme in his wonderful 1866 hymn:

The church's one foundation, is Jesus Christ her Lord;
She is His new creation, by water and the Word;

From heav'n He came and sought her, to be His holy Bride;
With His own blood He bought her and for her life He died.

Elect from every nation, yet one o'er all the earth;
Her charter of salvation, one Lord, one faith, one birth;
One holy name she blesses, partakes one holy food;
And to one hope she presses, with every grace endued.

Though with a scornful wonder, men see her sore oppressed;
By schisms rent asunder, by heresies distressed;
Yet saints their watch are keeping, their cry goes up, "How long?"
And soon the night of weeping, shall be the morn of song.

The church shall never perish! Her dear Lord to defend;
To guide, sustain, and cherish, is with her to the end;
Though there be those that hate her and false sons in her pale;
Against or foe or traitor, she ever shall prevail.

'Mid toil and tribulation, and tumult of her war;
She waits the consumation, of peace forever more;
Till with the vision glorious, Her longing eyes are blest;
And the great church victorious, shall be the church at rest.

Yet she on earth hath union, with God the three in one;
With mystic sweet communion, with those whose rest is won;
O happy ones and holy! Lord give us grace that we;
Like them, the meek and lowly, on high may dwell with thee.

I hope that as you proceed through this work that it may help you in some manner to be a wiser, more faithful and more joyful member, not only of your own local congregation, but also of that universal body of believers for whom Christ gave His life.

Curtis C. Thomas

Contents

Section One

Personal Responsibilities

OUR FIRST RESPONSIBILITY
Our Own Salvation!

"But now a righteousness from God, apart from law, has been made known, to which the Law and the Prophets testify. This righteousness from God comes through faith in Jesus Christ to all who believe" (Romans 3:21–22a).

At the age of seventeen I became a believer. It was the first time I had clearly understood the gospel. The spiritual light came on and I finally understood why Christ had died. Up to that point my theology was very fuzzy (actually, incorrect). Over a couple of weeks, in the spring of 1954, I realized that for me to be truly saved, to have my sins forgiven, to be justified before God, to be set right before an almighty and holy God, I must put my personal faith in Jesus Christ as my sin-bearer, the only One who *could take away* the awful guilt of my many sins.

At the age of nine I had joined a church, been immersed and had begun attending Sunday School and church services somewhat regularly. I would try to pray each night before going to sleep. I tried to live a moral, upright life. I was somewhat obedient to my parents and regularly prayed that they would not go to hell (they seldom attended church, especially my father). No individual ever asked me if I was saved, but should they have, I would have answered "yes." Yet, I often feared the torment of hell. I knew that I sinned and was constantly fearful that God would cast me into an everlasting fire. In those days farmers in our area would burn off their fields in the fall of the year. Just seeing those large fires would cause me severe mental and emotional anguish. I could picture myself in the middle of one of them calling on the rocks and hills to fall on me (at that time, more often than today, preachers gave "hell-fire and brimstone" sermons).

My reaction was to try to be more moral, to attend church services more frequently, to work harder on my Sunday School assignments, often lying awake at night fearing the imminent return of

Christ and my subsequent judgment. I cannot count the number of times I prayed that God would not cast me and my family into the endless torment of hell.

As I look back, I was trying to do what most people do: save myself by such things as baptism, church membership, prayer and morality.

But in the spring of 1954, God began a work of grace in my heart. A gentleman came to our home in an attempt to reach my brother who had joined a church cult. My brother would not meet with him (although my brother was saved almost ten years later). Instead, in God's gracious providence, the man approached me about teaching me the Scriptures. He asked if I could gather up some of my high school buddies for a class in our home. I was able to do so and in a short time, we began studying Romans. We had requested Revelation, but he was wise enough to steer us in the direction of a portion of the Scriptures that stressed the basics of the faith—Paul's letter to the Romans.

Within two weeks we came to Romans 1:16–17, "the just shall live by faith." God suddenly removed the scales from my eyes. I realized that my perspective on salvation had been totally wrong. It was not by morality, works, sincerity, church attendance or any other human merit or achievement. It was by grace, through faith in Christ as my substitute. The shock to my system turned out to be the salvation of my soul. It was as if I had believed all my life that the earth was flat and suddenly realized that it was a big round ball.

The burden was lifted and God's peace filled my soul. I knew that a righteous God had now adopted me into His family and that I would never have to face His wrath. Instead I learned that God had poured out His wrath upon His only Son in my place and that I was now saved eternally. My worldview was changed drastically. Later I realized what had taken place, that I had been born again by the powerful work of the Holy Spirit.

Obedience to God, church attendance and the study of the Scriptures now came to mean a way of life, not a way to obtain life. I understood my depravity and Satan's pull on me and why it was impossible to live a perfect life. I began to learn that the Holy Spirit was there to help me in my weaknesses and, though I was still a sinner, I had the finished work of Christ to atone for my sins. In addition, I was shown that the Spirit of God would help me in my feeble efforts to live the Christian life, to pray and to study God's Word. And I learned that my Lord was in heaven interceding for me.

What a tremendous relief! I learned that though I would spend the remainder of my days on this earth in a struggle with the world, my flesh and the Devil, yet I had now read the end of the book and knew that through Christ all of us who trust in Him would be "more than conquerors."

What about you? I assume that since you have picked up this book that you are probably a member of a local congregation. Perhaps you are a serious church member who wants to know what ministry you should engage in and what your responsibilities are. But of first importance, are you really a child of God? Have your sins been forgiven through the blood of Christ? Is He your Savior? Or, are you trying to save yourself by your own merits? Church membership? Baptism? Sincerity? Responsible lifestyle?

If so, just as I tried to earn my way into heaven, you are spiritually lost and are still accountable to God for your sins. Your first responsibility, therefore, in your journey to a ministry or church responsibility, must start at priority one—your own personal salvation. The Scriptures tell us to believe in the Lord Jesus Christ, to call on Him to save us and to trust in His work on the cross on our behalf (Acts 16:31; Romans 10:9–13). And John 6:37–40 makes it abundantly clear that whoever comes to Christ will never be driven away; that everyone who looks to the Son and believes in Him shall have eternal life and will be raised up at the coming of the Lord.

Paul, in Romans 12:1–3, instructs us that we are to be living sacrifices (servants of the Lord and of His church), but in order for us to be living sacrifices we must first be among the living—those who have been made alive (born again from above) through faith in Jesus Christ as our Lord and Savior. It is only at that point that we are on the road to acceptable service.

Application

For Individuals:

1. Read Romans 3:9–31 and 10:1–13. Summarize in one sentence what these verses are saying as to how to be saved.

2. What are you trusting in to get you to heaven?

3. List some evidences in your life which demonstrate that you have been born again by the Spirit of God.

For Groups:

1. What are some of the many ways by which people are trying to get to heaven?

2. Locate at least ten passages of Scripture in which the gospel method of salvation is clearly presented.

3. What are some of the better ways you have discovered to evangelize the lost?

4. Discuss some of the obstacles you have met in evangelizing and some of the ways you have overcome these obstacles.

Meditation

Prayerfully think through the meaning and implications of Romans 5:6–11.

OUR SECOND RESPONSIBILITY
Our Family's Salvation

"But as for me and my household, we will serve the Lord" (Joshua 24:15).

During my forty-plus years of ministry I have had the privilege of being around people who were serious about "soul-winning." I have listened to their sincere and earnest prayers for the salvation of their neighbors, co-workers, friends and classmates. I have seen them offer to work in visitation and "soul-winning" programs. I have attended witness-training classes with them. And I can testify to their deep desire to see others come to salvation through faith in Jesus Christ.

Yet, in some instances, regrettably, I have not seen the same earnestness for the members of their immediate family—a tremendous witnessing field with whom they have contact daily. God has graciously set each of us in the middle of this evangelistic field. Our families do see our sinful nature much more than strangers, making it hard for us to witness to them. Yet, God has placed us there and expects us to present the gospel to them regularly.

Make no mistake about it. God is the only one who saves. We cannot save anyone. But we can be the means which God uses to bring others to faith in His Son. Actually, we are the natural means for God to use in reaching our families. We must pray daily and fervently for them. Our lives must be a good example for them to follow. Our love for them should be genuine and sacrificial. We should encourage them about a serious study of the Word of God. We must seek to make it possible for them to participate in a solid, evangelical church. They should hear from us a clear presentation of the basics of the gospel. They must see a joyful attitude in us as we serve Christ and His people. Our entire lifestyle should be distinctly Christian. Our family standards must be based on clear biblical principles. Repentance, forgiveness, respect for authority and other Christian virtues should be both taught and exemplified.

It is wonderful for church members to want to evangelize the neighborhood. May there be a continuous army of such good people. But more basic than that is the need for evangelizing our own families. In the final analysis, our families are our strictest responsibility and will either be the occasion of our highest joy, or will bring to us our deepest regrets.

Application

For Individuals:

1. Does your private life before your family command respect?

2. Have you clearly explained the basics of the gospel to each member of your immediate family? Your extended family?

3. Do you regularly pray by name for the members of your family?

4. Make a list of those family members to whom you plan to present the gospel.

For Groups:

1. Discuss some of the ways you have found helpful in witnessing to your family members.

2. Discuss some of the ways that you have found that are not helpful in witnessing to your family members.

3. Provide the group with some names of your family members to whom you would like to witness and then pray as a group for their salvation.

Meditation

Prayerfully think through the meaning and implications of Ephesians 5:1–6:4 and 2 Timothy 1:5.

PERSONAL BIBLE STUDY

"… and how from infancy you have known the holy Scriptures, which are able to make you wise for salvation through faith in Christ Jesus. All Scripture is God-breathed and is useful for teaching, rebuking, correction, and training in righteousness…." (2 Timothy 3:15–16).

The apostle Paul is now in his final imprisonment in Rome, awaiting his execution. He writes to young Timothy to fan into flame the gift God had given him, to hold firm to the faith, to beware of false teachers and to preach the Word in season and out of season. He reminds Timothy that he had been brought up in the Scriptures by his grandmother, Lois and his mother, Eunice (see 2 Timothy 1:5). As Paul is about to pass off the scene, he passes the torch on to Timothy, the young man whom he describes as one who looks not after his own interests but those of others, knowing that he has a genuine interest in the spiritual welfare of the believers (see Philippians 2:19–23). Paul says he has no one else like Timothy. What a tremendous commendation coming from the great apostle Paul!

How did Timothy achieve such a glowing recommendation from this great apostle? While Paul certainly had much to do with it (as he took Timothy along on his journeys, teaching and modeling Christianity before him), Timothy's spiritual foundation began in his own home, as his grandmother and mother taught him the Scriptures. They had to have been thoroughly acquainted with the inspired Word of God (the Old Testament), which was able to teach, rebuke, correct and train one in righteousness.

While churches, Bible colleges and seminaries are very useful, the training must begin at home. And that requires us as parents to know the Bible ourselves if we are to pass God's Word on to our children. We can't depend solely upon the pastors, Sunday School teachers and others to train our families. That is our responsibility. And we cannot carry out that responsibility unless we, ourselves, are in the Word regularly.

There are many ways to study the Word of God. But here are some rather simple suggestions in case you have not embarked upon a program to thoroughly acquaint yourself with the Bible:

- Make sure that you own both a literal translation and a good paraphrase of the Scriptures.

- Build yourself a basic library of Bible helps (see the article included in this book on "Building a Personal Library").

- Plan to read the Bible through, from Genesis to Revelation, at least once a year. There are 1189 chapters in the Bible; covering approximately 3 chapters a day will get you through the Bible in a year. You may have time to go through it more than once a year.

- Choose an Old Testament book and a New Testament book in which to specialize each year. For the first year, I would recommend Genesis and either John or Romans.

- Read those two portions of the Bible over and over during the year. Once you think that you have a good grasp of what is in them, try to make your own outline of the contents.

- After you have gone through them a number of times and have completed your own outline, then begin to use some helps as follows:

  √ Read through a Bible survey which summarizes these books.

  √ Choose a good commentary to read on each book.

  √ Consult language helps on many of the important words the biblical writers use.

  √ Use a Bible handbook, a Bible Dictionary, a good Bible Atlas and a Bible encyclopedia to help you further understand names, events, doctrines, etc.

- Write down the general applications you have gleaned from your study of these passages. Then from that list, choose those applications on which you most need to work in your own life.

- Pay close attention to the context of each section or verse, always interpreting and applying a passage based on its context (otherwise, you may be interpreting the passage to teach one thing, whereas it may be teaching something totally different).

- Remember that Scripture is its own best interpreter. Compare other passages of Scripture where the subjects under study are being discussed.

- After you have completed your study of these two portions of Scripture, talk with others about what you have learned, to help ensure you have not gone astray on some issue.

- Then, next year start the cycle all over again, reading through the Bible verse by verse and then choosing another Old Testament and a New Testament book to study.

- Try to select a time of each day, when you are least distracted and most fresh, and commit yourself to a regular program of study.

- Do not attempt to go so fast that you skip right over important sections of the Bible.

You will be pleasantly surprised at how quickly you will become familiar with the Bible. While it will be tempting to initially choose a book like Revelation or Daniel, that is probably not a good place to start, especially if you are a new student in God's Word.

The Bible is a divinely inspired, inerrant and authoritative book and is truly useful and profitable for teaching, rebuking, correcting and training ourselves in righteousness. If we want sound, God-honoring churches we, the members, must be acquainted with the Scriptures. We cannot pass on the responsibility to our church leadership. Just as they must shepherd us so that we can carry out our individual ministries, we have an obligation to make certain that our churches and their leaders teach the Word of God accurately, requiring us to properly obey that Word.

Our most serious obligation is to our families, to bring them up in the fear and instruction of the Lord (Deuteronomy 6:4–9; Ephesians 6:4; Colossians 3:16). We cannot do that if we, ourselves, are not in the Word regularly.

Application

For Individuals:

1. Do you have a regular Bible study plan? Is it working?

2. Make an inventory of the helps you currently have and those which you need. (Again, consult the article in this book on "Building a Personal Library.")

3. You may want to ask your spouse, or another person, to consider staying on the same track with you so that you will have another person with whom to talk regularly as you study portions of the Word.

4. Keep in mind that the purpose of your study is not just to fill your head with knowledge, but rather to train yourself in obedience.

5. God is His own interpreter. Pray regularly for His help in arriving at His truth.

For Groups:

1. Discuss the methods of Bible study which each of you has found helpful.

2. Which translations do you use and why?

3. Which Bible study tools have you found to be particularly useful?

Meditation

Prayerfully think through the meaning and implications of 1 Timothy 4:1-5 and Revelation 22:18-20.

FAMILY WORSHIP

"Fathers, do not exasperate your children; instead, bring them up in the training and instruction of the Lord" (Ephesians 6:4).

Perhaps you have heard this statement: "The family that prays together, stays together." There is a lot of truth in that statement. One could probably also add, "The family that worships together, stays together." My experience bears out that those families who are regularly involved in a good church environment have a more solid foundation and support system than those who are without spiritual involvement. In many families, unfortunately, the church is basically the only source from which the family receives its spiritual nurture.

However, the New Testament does not place the primary responsibility upon the church to provide family worship. That responsibility rests with the father. He is to be the spiritual leader in his home. He may choose to delegate some aspects of the family worship to his wife and to the church, but the ultimate responsibility rests with him. The command in Ephesians 6:4 is specifically addressed to the fathers, who are the God-ordained leaders of the home.

Certainly part of his responsibility is to have his family actively participating in a good local church. This is one of the ways each family member can hear the gospel, grow spiritually and mature as a believer. But this spiritual nurturing must begin in the home.

Sadly, there are far too many spiritually passive fathers, who leave the responsibility of the spiritual upbringing of the children to the mothers. Often the mothers are the ones who pray with the children, discuss spiritual matters with them and see that the children are taken to church.

This is a sad state of affairs. Dad is charged to lead both his wife and children spiritually. He is to first lead by setting an example before his family by his walk before the Lord, by his prayers, by his Bible study and by his church involvement. Only as He is personally faithful to the Lord can he truly lead his family spiritually.

Then he is to lead his family by verbally teaching them. The best way to lead his family verbally in spiritual worship is to talk to them in all the natural settings God gives to him. He can discuss God's role in creation as he explores with them the natural world around them. As they learn of events in the world he can talk to them about how the Lord is not only the Creator but also the Sustainer and Controller of all events. When they see and experience the sinful world around them, he can talk to them about original sin and the effects of the fall of man. As they see hopelessness and despair among people, that can lead to discussions about how Christ came to redeem us from the curse and to bring about genuine hope. As they hear of people who have died, he can talk to them about the blessed hope of the resurrection. This type of spiritual instruction and leadership is an excellent means to reach the individual members of his family.

But there is also another dynamic in which he can corporately train and instruct his family—by collective family worship. There are some specific ways in which he can incorporate family worship in his household. Though each family will be different and each one will have its own schedule of activities, here are some suggestions of what can be done and what to avoid:

- Eliminate some activities which take up too much of the family's time and thus prevent family worship. There is nothing wrong with spending fun time with our families, but we do need to constantly examine our priorities to make sure that we are living in light of eternal realities.

- Choose a proper schedule. It may be impractical to plan a family worship time every day of the week. If so, perhaps two, three, or four times a week would be a better possibility. You may find that the evenings are better times to get the family together. The mornings can be a bit hectic in getting everyone off to school or work.

- Vary the contents. The actual worship time probably is more effective if the activities are varied from day to day, or week by week.

- Make the event meaningful. Some components might be: individual prayers, Bible reading, explanation of the passage (along with specific application), praise time for the Lord's goodness and for prayers answered, Bible memorization, biographical studies, missions concerns, Christian martyrs, discussing recent news events from a biblical perspective, even costumes or lessons with unusual visual aids, questions and comments, singing of familiar hymns or choruses and brief assignments to the family members for future worship times.

- If the children are small, some of the many good Bible storybooks could be read in which the interesting narratives of the Bible are covered. During those times the father could also provide additional details and interesting applications.

- Visual aids are very helpful and often will stimulate interest.

- Application of the truths covered should be brief, clear and on target.

- Involve each member. Encourage interesting and natural conversation back and forth among the family members during these times.

- In the Bible study portion, good interpretive and presentation skills must be followed. Passages should not be taken out of their context; otherwise the children will learn poor interpretive skills.

- Use a faithful, clear modern translation which the children can easily follow.

Here are some things to avoid in your family worship:

- Do not begin a session until family squabbles have been properly settled.

- The amount of time spent should be reasonable. Children will lose interest quickly and will begin to resent the entire session.

- Don't use the session as an opportunity to correct the children.

- Do not allow members to complain about each other during these times.

- Keep your prayers brief. Remember that children's attention spans are short.

- Do not embarrass family members. If you must deal with specific areas in their lives, do so individually and privately elsewhere.

Family worship can be wonderful experiences during which good, healthy spiritual relationships are built. Once you have started on such a program, stick to it. Vary the activities frequently and do not give up. Persevere in your plan, though you may not initially see positive results. Remember that you are embarking on a long-term goal. As a father, your responsibility as the spiritual leader of the family is to be faithful. The ultimate results are in the hands of Him who, alone, can bring about true spiritual change.

Application

For Individuals:

1. If you are not currently involved in a family worship program, begin making plans with your spouse to do so.

2. You may want to visit your local Christian bookstore to look for material on how to conduct a family worship time and materials to use during those times.

3. Ask your church leaders for their suggestions for family worship.

4. If you are currently involved in family worship, perhaps you could help others in your church to begin such a program.

For Groups:

1. Discuss ways in which you have conducted family worship.

2. Discuss ways to eliminate problems that can occur during these worship times.

3. Suggest materials which you have found helpful when conducting family worship.

Meditation

Prayerfully think through the meaning and implications of Romans 11:33–36.

GUARDING OUR MINDS

"Finally, brothers, whatever is true, whatever is noble, whatever is right, whatever is pure, whatever is lovely, whatever is admirable—if anything is excellent or praiseworthy—think about such things" (Philippians 4:8).

Scientists and medical personnel are now teaching us that what goes into our digestive system determines to a great extent our physical health. The wise person will eat those things which will help his body to work properly. Doing otherwise will eventually catch up with the person in the form of poor health.

The Scriptures warn us about putting the wrong things into our minds and about dwelling on such things. The mind is an extremely active organ. We are thinking about something most of our waking moments. And what we think about determines to a large extent what our spiritual health is like.

In the passage above, Paul instructs us to think about the right things—those things which are true, noble, right, pure, lovely, admirable, excellent, or praiseworthy. Those things will affect our attitudes and eventually, our walk before the Lord. To help understand what Paul was instructing us to do, I first want to look at it negatively and then consider its positive application.

First, some of the negatives which Paul wants us to *avoid*:

- Dwelling on immoral matters

- Developing a pessimistic attitude

- Thinking about injustices we have suffered

- Anger and resentment

- Talking about, or thinking about, the faults of others

- Comparing ourselves with others

- Covetous thoughts

- Planning revenge

- Selfish plans

- Crafting ways to make our own lives comfortable at the expense of others

- Seeking to get out of scriptural obligations

- Devising ways to cut others down, or to see them fail

- Thoughts of grandeur

This list could be extended to cover a number of areas in which we disobey these verses, but these are given to cause us to think about what Paul is writing against. A much longer list could be given to cover the positive things Paul wants our minds to dwell upon. Here are some things for us to *positively think about*:

- Our salvation (our calling, justification, sanctification, glorification)

- The complete forgiveness of all of our sins—past, present, future

- God's wonderful attributes

- God's tremendous promises to us

- The glories of Christ and His wondrous cross

- The power of the gospel

- The absolute security of our salvation

- The hope (a confident expectation) of the resurrection

- The plans to give us a new body, free from sickness, injury, decay

- The gift of the Holy Spirit

- The gifts of the Holy Spirit

- The church, universal and local

- God's providence and protection

- Christian brothers and sisters

- How we can help those who have fallen

- How we can support needy causes

- How we can use our gifts in the church

- The strength of God's mighty power

- God's physical provisions for us

- Ways to reach the lost

- Ways to reduce suffering in this world

- Ways to encourage the down-hearted

- Ways to encourage our fellow members and our church leadership

- New ways to make our church more responsive

- Ways to defeat sin in our lives

- Ways to draw closer to God

This list could go on and on for pages. There should be so many good things going on in the Christian's life that if we dwelt upon them, there would be little time to concentrate on the rotten things of this world. The short verses that we have heard and sung on many occasions sums up very practically how we can obey Paul's words:

> Count your many blessings;
> Name them one by one;
> Count your many blessings;
> And see what God has done.

Though quite simple, these words are very profound. They are a call to meditate on God's goodness to us. That is the answer to negative thinking, pessimism, depression, anger, resentment, bitterness and all of the other things which dwell in our minds. Those things fail the test of being true, noble, right, pure, lovely, admirable, or praise-worthy.

Harness your mind to this thought: "I sincerely deserve to be thrown into hell. Yet God has freely given me an eternity in heaven through the sacrifice of his own Son. He has promised that He loves me and that He will never leave me nor forsake me. I am His forever." If your mind is constantly captive to these awesome truths, you can't be dwelling on the filth and the vain thinking of this present world.

Application

For Individuals:

1. What are some of the associations you have, some of the TV programs you watch, some of the books or magazines you read, which you need to give up today?

2. What are some of the good things which you need to substitute for the above?

3. If you have any unfinished business (such as granting forgiveness to another, or correcting any wrong you have committed), make plans to tend to those matters as quickly as possible.

For Groups:

1. Locate other portions of Scripture which speak to us about what goes into our minds.

2. What are some of our society's subtle influences against which we need to guard?

3. Talk about ways which you find helpful to keep your mind on wholesome and godly thoughts.

Meditation

Prayerfully think through the meaning and implications of Galatians 5:19–26, Romans 8:5–11, and Philippians 1:27–2:18.

ATTITUDE
A MOST IMPORTANT INGREDIENT

"About midnight Paul and Silas were praying and singing hymns to God, and the other prisoners were listening to them" (Acts 16:25).

It has been said that the way a person looks at a rose bush determines whether he is an optimist or a pessimist. A pessimist is sad that rose bushes have thorns. An optimist is delighted that thorn bushes have roses. Our attitudes, or perspectives, are extremely important and often will determine how effectively we can witness.

The context surrounding the verse quoted above from Acts 16 contains Paul's and Silas' witness in Philippi. After Paul and Silas had cast out an evil spirit from a slave girl, the owners of the girl dragged Paul and Silas before the authorities with trumped-up charges. The crowds joined in the attack against these two godly men, after which the authorities had them stripped, beaten and severely flogged. Then, without any medical attention to their severe wounds, and though they were Roman citizens, they were thrown into the jail where they were placed in the inner cell. Their feet were placed in the stocks—a device that caused severe pain.

Even though they were publicly humiliated and were in intense pain, Paul and Silas were praying and singing hymns. The other prisoners were listening. No doubt they were wide-eyed as Paul and Silas, rather than complaining and threatening to retaliate against their accusers or the authorities, were praising God through their prayers and hymn-singing. Suddenly, God miraculously delivered them by an earthquake. In the process the jailer, his family and possibly even some of the fellow prisoners were saved through the gospel testimony of Paul and Silas.

Paul's and Silas' attitudes (or perspectives) were an important ingredient in their testimony. Had they been grumbling, complaining, even cursing their situation, nobody would have listened to them. But instead, they were doing what Peter urged his readers to do when he wrote: "In this you greatly rejoice, though now for a little while you may have suffered grief in all kinds of trials" (1 Peter 1:6). Peter's readers had been dispersed because of persecution and had lost all things—their homes, their jobs, their worldly possessions and, in many cases, their families. Like them, we are also called to rejoice even when we are suffering.

Our attitudes (or perspectives) are very important ingredients in our Christian walk. They not only affect our own outlook but also those of our families, our co-workers, our friends and neighbors, our fellow church members and the lost whom we hope to evangelize. If our outlook is pessimistic or dismal, people simply do not want to be around us, much less listen to us. If we exhibit a genuine optimism and a joyful spirit, people will be attracted to our testimony.

A number of years ago I learned a phrase from a young man who was an energetic witness of the gospel. When people nonchalantly asked him, "How are you?" he would always answer, "Much better than I deserve," meaning that he was living joyfully under God's grace. I now answer people who ask me that question the same way. It has led to a number of brief discussions about the Lord's wonderful grace and mercy. When one answers that question with, "OK, considering the circumstances," or "I could be better," or "Alright, I guess," an opportunity is missed. An answer with a genuine, Christ-honoring statement of some sort can generate both a rich testimony and a setting in which to discuss God's wonderful gift of grace.

However, it is not just the response to a greeting with which we are concerned—it is our overall attitude. If we are truly children of God, we have so much about which to be thankful and to rejoice. Our sins have been eternally forgiven. Our home is heaven. Someday we will share God's glory. Our trials and difficulties in this life will soon end. Sin will be totally eradicated when we get to heaven. God is our loving Father. His grace will sustain us. His arms of protection are surrounding us. He has given us loving brothers and sisters in the Lord. Even our sufferings are here to develop character and, subsequently, hope—and we know that in the end we will win with Christ.

There is no end to God's graciousness toward us. How can we help but rejoice? Paul reminds us of this throughout the letter to the Philippians. He summarizes his thoughts by a command in chapter

4, verse 4, where he says, "Rejoice in the Lord always. I will say it again: Rejoice!"

How can we make this joy apparent in our lives and, especially, in our local church bodies? Here are some practical suggestions:

- Make a habit of verbally expressing your gratitude to the Lord for His choosing you to be one of His children.

- Express your optimism that God has *all* things in control and that He is working *all* things together for the spiritual good of His children.

- Be willing to optimistically accept your responsibilities in your local church. If you are needed on the construction crew, volunteer willingly. If you are needed on the clean-up crew, or needed in the nursery, or needed as a teacher, express your joy at being able to serve Christ in that way.

- If problems occur in your church body, rather than complaining, seek to help in a God-honoring way to bring about a solution or resolution.

- Never complain about others. Use your tongue to build up others, rather than tearing them down.

- Pass along to others your gratitude and joy when good things are happening. Good attitudes are helped along by positive enthusiasm. (Remember that bad attitudes are also passed along to others.)

- Let people know that you are praying for them. The church staff especially needs this. Often they receive more criticism than verbal support. A word or note of positive encouragement can mean much to them.

- As you are around the lost, be especially mindful of the ways you express your attitudes. Many of them live in a dismal, dog-eat-dog world where there is little hope or joy. Brighten their days with a genuine, helpful, positive outlook. That may help attract them to your Lord. Paul instructs us to make the doctrines of our Lord attractive (Titus 2:10).

Our perspectives matter. In our church for many years we held an annual Christmas banquet during which we had a fun time, usually including some Christian entertainment. It was an occasion when the congregation expressed gratitude to the staff and a time of joyful fellowship. At one year's banquet, a church member had invited a lost friend. After the banquet, that lost friend went back to his home where, unable to sleep, he pondered and mulled over what he had witnessed. Finally, at 2:00 AM, he awakened his Christian friend with a phone call, in which he said "I don't know what you folks have, but whatever it is, I want it." Our member explained to him that it came through a personal commitment and relationship with the Lord Jesus Christ. As the member witnessed to him, the Holy Spirit opened the man's heart and he was gloriously saved.

This wonderful story began with the members of our church collectively expressing joy as they fellowshipped together. This man knew that his life was empty and joyless and he finally saw something much better.

We, Christians, have the best of the best—the good news of a gospel that works! Let's express it everywhere and always—by our words and by our perspectives.

Application

For Individuals:

1. In what areas do you need to improve your attitude?

2. Encourage others close to you to help hold you accountable for your attitudes.

3. What can you do to help the general attitudes of your fellow church members?

4. Memorize this phrase: "As a Christian I must develop and express an *attitude of gratitude.*"

For Groups:

1. Discuss some bad attitudes that you have seen expressed among Christians (without naming individuals).

2. Discuss ways in which you can help your own attitude and that of your fellow church members.

3. What are some other things, other than those listed above, which should have a positive effect on our attitudes?

Meditation

Prayerfully think through the meaning and implications of Philippians 1:15–18 and 4:10–13.

BE A BARNABAS
AN ENCOURAGER

"Therefore encourage each other with these words" (1 Thessalonians 4:18).

God works through men to achieve great ministries. Barnabas was one of those men. When Saul (Paul) was gloriously converted on the Damascus road and called to be God's special messenger (an apostle) to the Gentile world, the Christian brothers were at first afraid of him. And that was understandable. Prior to his calling by Christ, Paul had been a relentless persecutor of the early church. He committed people to prison and even to death. Those early leaders evidently thought Paul was up to some of his old tricks and so they were afraid of him. Neither could they understand his plans to evangelize the Gentiles.

It took Barnabas "going to bat" for Paul to assure the Jerusalem brothers that Paul was now truly a believer in Christ and to encourage the brothers to give Paul their fellowship and support of his ministry (Acts 9:26–30). Barnabas was simply living up to his name—"son of encouragement."

We also see Barnabas being used as an encourager to young John Mark early in his life. After John Mark had deserted Paul and Barnabas in their first journey, Paul felt it best not to include one who had turned back. The Scriptures tell us that Barnabas and Paul had a strong dispute over John Mark (Acts 15:37–41). It was settled with Paul departing on his second journey with Silas, while Barnabas took young John Mark along with him to Cyprus (where history records that the gospel did penetrate that island, evidently through the ministries of Barnabas and Mark).

Finally, at the close of the apostle Paul's ministry, Paul sends for Mark, stating that he was now "useful" to him (2 Timothy 4:11).

One could wonder what might have happened to Mark had he been left alone with no encourager to come alongside him. The Scriptures do not tell us who was right or wrong in Barnabas and

Paul's dispute. Perhaps both were right. Paul could have correctly judged that Mark was not yet ready for such a rigorous trip. Perhaps Barnabas correctly assumed that, with his assistance to Mark, the young man could later prove to be a capable and dedicated servant of Christ.

In both of these situations, the "son of encouragement" lived up to his name.

The New Testament calls on all of us who are believers to "encourage one another" (1 Thessalonians 4:18; Hebrews 10:25). The exercise of this gift is needed in the body of Christ. Some among us are especially gifted in this area, but all of us are responsible to encourage each other. Here are some of the possible ways:

- Encourage the leadership by written, verbal and prayer support.

- Encourage the leadership and membership by your faithful and regular financial support.

- Encourage those with special gifts or abilities to use them to the fullest for the good of the body.

- Use whatever gifts and talents God has given you for the body.

- Ask for the opportunity to serve; don't wait until you are approached.

- Encourage the sick by visiting or calling them regularly; pray for and with them.

- Encourage the body by faithfully attending the services and ministries—with punctuality.

- Encourage the leadership and membership by exhibiting a genuine, positive outlook.

- Refrain from criticizing the leaders and other members.

- Verbally encourage people to trust in their sovereign God who loves them, who knows all things and who controls all things for their good.

- Exhibit this same trust yourself when hurtful events occur in your life.

- Know the Scriptures and encourage others with the words of Scripture.

- When a death occurs, encourage others by talking about the blessed hope we have in the resurrection.

- Encourage those who are just starting out in teaching and preaching by pointing out that with God's help as they exercise that gift, they will improve.

- Encourage other members to support the church leadership and ministries.

- Speak positively about other worthwhile ministries within the body.

- Share with others about someone within the body who has been a blessing in your life.

- Like Barnabas, regularly carry out an encouraging discipleship with a new believer.

- Share information about answered prayers.

- Send notes of encouragement and appreciation for gifts exercised in the body.

- Be the first to volunteer for needed ministries.

- Offer to help people with particular and special needs.

- If able, anonymously provide financial help to those members who cannot afford to attend special seminars, retreats, conferences, mission trips, etc.

- Write encouraging letters to those members who live alone and to those missionaries who are serving faithfully and, often, alone.

Application

For Individuals:

1. Name some individuals who have encouraged you.

2. In what ways have other Christians discouraged you?

3. Of the suggestions above, which ones (or additional ones) do you plan to put into practice this month?

For Groups:

1. What are some of the causes of spiritual discouragement among Christians?

2. Discuss ways in which Christians can discourage others.

3. Discuss some examples where other Christians have encouraged you.

4. What are some of the harms that can occur when a Christian is lacking in encouragement?

Meditation

Prayerfully think through the meaning and implications of Philippians 1:3–11.

PRAYER
PRIVATE AND PUBLIC

"When you pray, go into your room, close the door and pray to your Father, who is unseen. Then your Father, who sees what is done in secret, will reward you. And when you pray, do not keep on babbling like pagans, for they think they will be heard because of their many words…. If you, then, though you are evil, know how to give good gifts to your children, how much more will your Father in heaven give good gifts to those who ask him" (Matthew 6:6–7; 7:11).

The Bible is replete with examples, commands and encouragements to us to be involved in prayer. In fact, the topic is brought up so often in Scripture that we could not begin to adequately cover the subject in such a short space. Therefore our approach will, of necessity, have to be severely limited, somewhat arbitrary and will bring up only a few of the many aspects of prayer. What I want us to think about are some of the proper approaches to prayer. In doing so, we will list some of the most common misunderstandings regarding prayer.

- Prayer should recognize that God is omnipotent. He is all-powerful. When we pray to God it is with the assumption that God has the ability to do whatever He pleases, when He pleases and how He pleases. To believe otherwise is to dishonor the Person we are addressing and it gives our prayers a hollow ring. To not believe in a totally sovereign God is to pray insincerely or at best, inconsistently. How can we ask Him to do both ordinary and amazing things in answer to our prayer when we do not think He has the ability to do so?

- Prayer must involve praising, not simply asking God. Our prayers are too often self-centered. Much of our time spent in prayer is asking, but little in worship. In the "Lord's Prayer" (which is by its nature the *Disciples Prayer*, since Christ was teaching His disciples how to pray—Matthew 6:5–15), the first half is spent in praise and worship of God. Only the last portion addresses personal needs.

- Prayer is recognizing that God knows best. When we lay our needs before our Father we must leave the matter up to His omniscience. He alone knows whether the answer should be "yes", or "no", "not now", or "not in the way you want it." The answers, while specific needs must be mentioned, must be left to God's wisdom, not ours.

- Prayer is asking, not instructing or demanding. When listening to some people pray, it almost sounds as if God is on their payroll or in their debt and must jump to action when they pray. Often God is given very specific steps to take and timetables in which to answer their prayers. At other times it almost appears as if the person praying is trying to give a child directions as to how this prayer must be answered.

- Prayer is not a "name it, claim it" exercise. God has never promised to give us all of our desires. Many of them are sinful wants. He has promised to supply all of our spiritual *needs* in Christ Jesus, but not all of our *greeds*. It is insulting to God to so pray that we think He is obligated to give us what we want, when we want it, simply because we have named it and claimed it. That is not prayer; it is expecting God to fulfill our orders.

- Prayer should primarily be concerned with spiritual matters. It would probably be very revealing if we were to enumerate all of the things we ask for and then to eliminate all of those requests that were outside of our spiritual welfare. Our diagnosis would surely reveal that we are much more concerned with present comforts than those things which would most conform us to Christ Jesus.

- Prayer should primarily be in secret. There is a definite place for public prayer. And when God answers a public prayer, He can be publicly praised. But in the passage above, the clear teaching is that for the most part, our prayers should be private. The real intent of our hearts can best be laid out in private. In public, often the words used and the way things are stated are intended to impress those who are listening. But in private we have only one audience—God. And in those times all façade has been done away with and there is nothing between our God and us.

- Public prayer is exemplified and taught in the Bible, but it must be done properly. It must not be uttered in order to be heard by men and, as our passage indicates, must not be lengthy, rambling and prayed in a way which draws attention to ourselves. When prayer is given in that manner, God is definitely neither pleased nor glorified.

- Prayer is not to turn into a public gossip session. Sometimes confidential matters are brought up in public prayers. Or God is often called upon during prayer to deal with certain individuals regarding their sins. These matters should not be mentioned publicly. Yet, somehow, since we are talking to God, it seems that it is permissible to mention these things. God is displeased when this occurs. Gossip is gossip, whether it appears in our discussions or in our prayers.

- Answers to prayer can surprise us. For example, in Romans 5, Paul makes it clear that the way to Christian character is through suffering. If we pray for character, God is going to answer consistently with His revealed Word—and that will be through suffering. If we were to pray for patience, God may answer that prayer by placing us in difficult situations that will require us to learn to exercise patience.

- Promises to pray about matters must be taken seriously. Often we are asked to pray for certain things and we assure the person that we will do so. Then we promptly forget it. That should not occur. Perhaps the best way is, when possible, to stop right then and there to pray about the matter. Or, perhaps we should jot it down in a notebook to remind us that we have made that commitment.

- We must never exaggerate any prayer request or prayers answered. God always knows the truth and we must state things to Him in truth. And when God answers a prayer we must always tell the truth about how He answered our prayer. In this regard, God's name is often blasphemed by TV evangelists and preachers who claim miraculous things in answer to prayer, when in many cases there is no truth to the claim whatsoever. We must acknowledge that God does not always give us what we want. He would be a very poor father who fulfilled every request of his children.

- When it is clear that God has answered a prayer, we must praise Him for it. This can be done both privately and publicly. But it must be done in such a way as to give all the praise to God, rather than trying to steal some of the praise. We must never leave the impression that we were so important that God had to answer our prayer in the specific way in which our request was presented.

There are many other things, which could be said about the necessity of prayer, the form of our prayers, the things about which we should pray, the many examples and principles of prayer, but space will not permit us to do so. Our purpose here has been to try to correct some of the mistakes and excesses committed by well-meaning Christians who pray. It is true that "we have not because we ask not" (James 4:2) and that we must pray fervently and unceasingly (James 5:16; Luke 18:1–8). We cannot pray enough. We have great spiritual needs. If the Lord Jesus Christ had to demonstrate His dependence upon the Father by prayer, how much more you and I need to daily commune with our Heavenly Father about a whole host of issues. God wants to have regular communication with us. He talks to us through the Bible and we talk with Him through prayer. How sad it is when the children seldom talk with their Father.

Application

For Individuals:

1. In what specific ways can you rearrange your daily schedule to get in more time for serious spiritual reflection and prayer?

2. What are some of the areas in your life, in your family, in your area of influence and in your church that you need to be addressing in prayer?

3. Jot down some significant answers to prayer you have experienced. Then regularly praise God for both His character and for His granting your requests.

For Groups:

1. What are some inappropriate ways that public prayers can be conducted?

2. What are some good methods you could suggest by which prayer needs might be expressed to your church body?

3. Often answered prayer is described by Christians as a "miraculous" event.   Discuss what are truly miraculous answers to prayer and what are ordinary.

4. It is apparent that God does not always give us what we ask for. Discuss why that is true.

Meditation

Prayerfully think through the meaning and implications of Philippians 4:6–7.

CHURCH FINANCES
OUR PART

"Command those who are rich in this present world not to be arrogant nor to put their hope in wealth, which is so uncertain, but to put their hope in God, who richly provides us with everything for our enjoyment. Command them to do good, to be rich in good deeds, and to be generous and willing to share. In this way they will lay up treasure for themselves as a firm foundation for the coming age, so that they may take hold of the life that is truly life" (1 Timothy 6:17–19).

Some have categorized our Lord's teaching in various ways and have come up with the following statement: The Lord talked about our money and possessions more than any other individual subject. To say the least, there is more material in the New Testament about our money and possessions than we relish obeying. Some significant examples are: Matthew 5:42; 6:19–21, 25–34; 19:16–24; Luke 12:13-21; Acts 2:44-45; 4:32–35; Philippians 4:12-13; 1 Timothy 6:6–10; Revelation 3:17–19.

Some basic principles about our money and possessions are:

- The Lord owns *everything*. We are merely stewards over His holdings for a brief period of time.

- The Lord expects us to invest these means in His kingdom.

- We are to be shrewd in the management of what the Lord has placed into our care.

- We are to be generous and cheerful givers.

- We are to support the local church.

- We are to support other godly causes.

- God will bless those who handle their possessions with wisdom and generosity.

- God will withhold from those who are selfish and foolish.

- There will be a day of reckoning in which we will be held responsible for the manner in which we have used our resources.

While other principles can be gleaned from the Scripture, these alone should cause us to be honest and diligent with those things over which God had made us temporary managers.

One question members often ask their pastor is: "How much should I give?" In other words, "What is enough?" Sometimes it appears that the question behind the question may be "How little can I give in order to have a clear conscience?"

In the American church scene we have very few people who know what it means to give sacrificially. On several occasions I have taught a Christian Financial Principles class and when doing so have explained that *sacrificial giving* meant that you "gave until it hurts." After one of the more recent classes, an elderly lady respectfully challenged that definition of sacrificial giving. To her *sacrificial giving* is when a person gives until it hurts and then *keeps on giving*. I had to admit that her definition seemed more in line with the New Testament spirit of giving than mine. I now use her definition.

Obviously a church requires money. Pastors need salaries. Buildings require construction costs, maintenance, utilities and other expenditures. Missionaries need support. Youth ministries have expenses. The money must come from somewhere. In the Old Testament when God dropped manna from heaven, the Levitical priests still had to be supported by the Israelites. And so the proper question which should be asked by church members is, "What does the Lord want me to give?"

Some would answer with a percentage—a 10% tithe. Yet, when one looks carefully into the Scriptures it is clear that the tithe was an Old Testament theocratic income tax. And when you study the subject carefully, the Old Testament tithe was really 23 1/3% (some would calculate it at 33 1/3%). In the New Testament the 10% tithe is mentioned only three times and in those instances it is never a command (Matthew 23:23 [repeated in Luke 11:42]; Luke 18:12; Hebrews 7:4–9). Thus, under the New Testament there is no set percentage required for all believers alike. For some, 10% may be reasonable, but it should never be imposed on members as a New Testament requirement. For others 2% might be fair and for some members with tremendous wealth, 80% might be reasonable. No set percentage is stipulated in the New Testament.

But, there are New Testament guidelines. Here are some of the more important ones. We are to give:

- In response to God's love (2 Corinthians 9:15), after having first given ourselves (2 Corinthians 8:5).

- Of the first fruits (1 Corinthians 16:1).

- Trusting God (2 Corinthians 9:8–10).

- With a view toward eternity (Matthew 6:19–20).

- Without desire for personal recognition (Matthew 6:1–4).

- As the Lord has prospered us (2 Corinthians 8:11–12).

- Generously (2 Corinthians 9:6–7).

- Cheerfully (2 Corinthians 8:1–7; 9:7.

- Systematically (1 Corinthians 16:1).

- According to the need (2 Corinthians 8:13–15).

- Following Christ's pattern of sacrifice (2 Corinthians 8:9; Hebrews 12:2–3).

By honestly and realistically using the above principles (plus others gleaned from the Scriptures), coupled with prayer to God for guidance, each church member should be able to determine what his fair share should be in order to support the church and her ministries.

One last word of advice: Should you still have serious questions about what you should give, seek counsel from some godly members of your own body (perhaps the leadership) and ask for their advice and guidance. Proverbs tells us clearly that there is wisdom in the godly counsel of others (12:15; 13:10; 19:20–21; 20:18)—and that certainly can apply to the stewardship of our money.

Application

For Individuals:

1. Are you giving regularly to support your church?

2. Are you satisfied that you are giving your fair share?

3. If not, list below the names of church leaders or members with whom you plan to discuss your financial stewardship in order to help you determine how much you should give.

For Groups:

1. What are some of the excuses Christians use that prevent their giving sacrificially?

2. What are some of the things about which we should think in connection with giving?

3. How does one decide how much of his giving should be divided among the church's general fund, the building fund, the benevolence fund, the mission fund and other needs in our society?

4. What are some of the things a Christian can do when his living expenses eat up his entire paycheck and he has nothing left to give to the Lord?

5. If a Christian has obligations or debts, should he use some of that money to give to the Lord's work, or should he pay off those debts first?

Meditation

Prayerfully think through the meaning and implications of Philippians 4:19 and 1 Timothy 6:17–19.

FRIENDSHIP WITH THE WORLD

"I have written you in my letter not to associate with sexually immoral people—not at all meaning the people of this world who are immoral, or the greedy and swindlers, or idolaters. In that case you would have to leave this world" (1 Corinthians 5:9–10).

The Bible has much to say about the *world*. In many cases it refers to the world of lost sinners. We are given much instruction about not being a part of this *world* and keeping ourselves unstained from the *world*. James even says that "friendship with the world is hatred toward God" (James 4:4). And yet we must live in the world, as Paul notes in the verse quoted above. And if we are going to see the world saved, someone must associate with the world to take the gospel.

Therein lies a paradox. We must go into the world, but not be a part of the world. Even the apostle Paul said that he became all things to all men so that by doing so he might save some (1 Corinthians 9:22). The question is: how does one become all things to all men without being a friend to the world—in the sense that James was talking about?

Often I hear people rejoicing about moving into a neighborhood where all of their neighbors are Christians, or of securing a job where all of their co-workers are believers. My response usually is to express disappointment. While it is enjoyable to work and fellowship with believers, there is a simple truth that we must face: Christians do not become Christians. Only the lost members of the world can *become* Christians. And when we cut ourselves off from interaction with the lost, we restrict our Christian witness.

What James and other New Testament writers are talking about is becoming such a part of the world that our thinking and our morals are polluted. We do that when we subtly value what they value, think like they think, respond like they respond, act like they act, use resources like they use theirs and refuse to talk to them about the gospel and its demands.

But there is a good sense in which we should become a friend to the world. And the purpose is to get the gospel to them in order to save them out of the world, hoping to see them go back into the world to reach others who are still a part of the world. There are no better examples than those of our Lord and of the apostle Paul. They went where the lost were—to the temple, to the synagogues, to the market, to the riverbank, to the wicked cities, to the boats—so that they could meet and talk to people.

In the verse quoted above from 1 Corinthians 5, Paul is instructing us not to associate with a professing believer who is living in a state of unrepentant sin. To make sure that the Corinthians understood, he explains that he is not talking about the world of lost sinners. We have to associate with them, because that is the world in which we live. But it is also the world in which we must witness.

We definitely need Christian friends. But we also need to make friends with the lost, in order to reach them for the gospel. Obviously, we must not fall into their lifestyle, but should use every opportunity available to show them by our life and to tell them by our tongue, just what Christ means to us. Opportunities are all around us; we just need to cultivate an eye for the best means available in meeting and influencing these people.

There is *no one correct way* to evangelize. It will vary from person to person and from situation to situation. God has indeed blessed evangelistic or revival meetings, formal evangelistic programs, lifestyle evangelism, the distribution of books, tracts, other literature and many other ways of reaching the lost. In my own experience, friendship evangelism seems to work best for me, coupled later with a Bible study of some kind. Here are some of the ways to meet new people, to form friendships with them, to earn their confidence and then to have the opportunity to talk to them about their souls:

- Make a list of your extended family and concentrate on those who are lost.

- Plan to spend time doing a variety of things with them. Let them know that you really care for them; earn the right to talk to them.

- Do the same for your neighbors. Get to know them and determine what interests you have in common with them. Help them with a chore; invite them over for a meal or refreshments; take them on a picnic, campout, golf outing. etc.

- Invite some of your co-workers to your home, or to some outing where you can show them that you have an interest in them other than at work.

- Join an organization which regularly puts you in contact with other people. It could be a scout program, an exercise gym, a softball team, a hunting club, a civic club, a hobby group, or any other entity which regularly puts you in contact with people with whom you would not ordinarily have contact.

There are many other avenues for meeting new people. Meeting others gives you the opportunity to become a "friend to the world" so that by the gospel, you might win some out of the world.

Your personality, their personalities, the effort you put into it, the time you are able to spend and the individual situations will determine how successful you are in forging those friendships. But keep in mind that God is able to make things work even when we think they are hopeless. He is calling on FAST people to do his work: Faithful, Available, Service-oriented, Teachable. Make yourself available, work at it faithfully and keep trying to learn. Ask God to help you make those friendships, then ask Him to bless your life and your tongue as you model and talk about Christ to these new friends.

Once you have made some new friends, try to involve them in a Bible study of some type, or a worthwhile discipleship program. Inviting them to church at first is not always the best method. They may feel more comfortable at first in a one-on-one study, or perhaps a home Bible study. As interest grows and if the Lord saves them, they will probably take the initiative at that point. Ultimately you will want to see them active in a sound Bible-teaching church where they can grow as Christians.

Application

For Individuals:

1. What new areas can you think of right now where you can meet new people?

2. Do you have a close Christian friend whom you could ask to join with you in trying to create new circles of friends? Our Lord sent men out two by two. Another person can encourage us and can help hold us accountable. List some names at this point.

3. Do you currently have some lost friends? List them and try to think of the best way to get them into a discipleship program or Bible study.

For Groups:

1. Discuss specific ways in which you can violate the biblical principle of not being a friend to the world.

2. Discuss ways to become friends with new people in order to evangelize them.

3. In your own group, think about choosing a partner to hold you accountable and to help in evangelizing others.

4. In the group, pray about some specific individuals with whom you would like to become better acquainted in order to bring the gospel to them.

Meditation

Prayerfully think through the meaning and implications of Romans 10:14–15.

TRUST
ALWAYS THE STARTING POINT

"It [love] always protects, always trusts, always hopes, always perseveres" (1 Corinthians 13:7).

This verse is describing some of the characteristics of love. It is set in the context of instructions to the Corinthians who were exercising spiritual gifts in their worship services. In the middle of his correcting words, Paul pauses to remind the Corinthians of the three greatest gifts—faith, hope and love. His conclusion is that love is the greatest of all the gifts. Charles Hodge, in his commentary on 1 Corinthians, says that love is the greatest because it is the most useful. Love has application for all people for all times. In that sense, love is the most useful. It helps the most.

In verse 7, Paul points out that one of the characteristics of love is that we trust others, especially in the local church. Paul says that love always trusts.

We know that people come into this world guilty of Adam's sin, are born with a sinful nature and have a propensity toward sin. As long as we are in this life, we will never be totally free of sin. However, we have been given the Holy Spirit who is busy in us with His sanctifying work, which will not be totally completed until we reach heaven. There is no one who can be trusted to do all the right things, at all times, with completely right motives. Only Christ could live free of sin. Yet, here is Paul telling us that love always trusts.

What is Paul saying to us? He is telling us to start out with fellow believers by trusting them—their words and their motives. That is how genuine love acts. We must refuse to believe any ill report of our fellow believers until irrefutable proof is given.

This is extremely important in the local church. Gossip and rumors float easily and can destroy a reputation of a pastor, officer, or member of a local congregation. As rumors travel around, people sometimes take them in and then send them out to others. Often additional unfounded accusations are added so that before long the story does not even resemble the original. But unfortunately, some people believe the story without ever checking to see if the accusations are true. When that happens, Paul's words have been clearly violated.

Love trusts or believes the best about a friend, neighbor or fellow church member until clear proof has been presented otherwise. If this principle were followed, many whose good names have been soiled by the rumor mill—even in a local church, would never have to face ugly accusations and spend time and energy restoring their reputations. This is particularly true about pastors and other church leaders. One single, unfounded accusation can ruin their reputations for life. Often these charges are never made public, but continually float around the church for years, much like a feather floating in the wind.

Our local bodies would be so much more blessed and happy if we Christians followed Paul's admonition: Love always trusts. Love never is suspicious of others. It never passes along a rumor. It does not look for the bad in others. Instead, it protects. It looks for that which is right and just and lovely. It seeks to protect the reputation of others and to build them up, rather than tearing them down. It refuses to believe a rumor, a bad report, or to pass along something negative about another, unless and until the matter is beyond question and it is biblically appropriate to do so. The apostle Peter says that "love covers a multitude of sins" (1 Peter 4:8). Love refuses to pass on to others anything that does not edify others or bring glory to God.

Application

For Individuals:

1. Have you believed the worst about a fellow member without ever knowing the real facts?

2. Are there rumors currently floating around about a fellow church member or official which you need to help squelch?

3. What could you be doing in your church to help 1 Corinthians 13:7 to be obeyed?

For Groups:

1. Discuss instances (without naming individuals) in which Christians violate this aspect of love (trusting others).

2. Does 1 Corinthians 13:7 require of us that we always trust others, regardless of evidence which would cause us to do otherwise?

3. Christ told us to be as wise as serpents and as innocent as doves. How should these two principles be applied in our lives as we try to obey 1 Corinthians 13:7?

Meditation

Prayerfully think through the meaning and implications of Philippians 2:1–11.

OUR WORK MATTERS TO GOD

"Slaves, obey your masters in everything; and do it, not only when their eye is on you and to win their favor, but with sincerity of heart and reverence for the Lord. Whatever you do, work at it with all of your heart, as working for the Lord, not for men, since you know that you will receive an inheritance from the Lord as a reward. It is the Lord Christ you are serving" (Colossians 3:22–24).

Sometimes in their zeal to encourage spiritual vocations, pastors can unintentionally leave the impression among church members that unless one is in some form of full-time gospel work (such as a pastor, missionary or evangelist) that other forms of vocation are less spiritual, or of less importance to God. As a result many Christians do not seem to grasp how important it is for them to serve their employers with submission and excellence, as a way to bring glory to God. This misunderstanding is further highlighted by the use of the terms religious and secular vocations. The biblical position is that all work matters to God, whether one serves as a pastor, or sits at a computer eight hours per day, or engages as an evangelist, or works as a diesel mechanic.

In the passage above Paul reminded the slaves in Colossae that their service to God was bound up in the manner in which they served their earthly masters. They were to work hard, serving with all of their hearts, rendering excellent service because ultimately that was their way of being obedient to their heavenly Master. Peter, in his first letter (2:18–19), tells slaves that they are to be obedient to their earthly masters, even those who are "harsh" (lit., morally crooked, perverse). In our culture, the slaves are equivalent to employees, and the masters are the employers or bosses—so these biblical commands are totally relevant in our age.

Whether we work as a convenience store clerk, a supervisor of hundreds of employees, or repair flat tires as our vocation, our attitude and performance on our jobs are critical ways to serve the

Lord and often determine how effective we are in our witness to the lost world around us. Realizing that all work is holy to God is a key ingredient in our being pleasing to the Lord. God is equally as concerned with our attitude and example whether we repair broken plumbing pipes, trade stock on a brokerage floor, lead a Bible class at church, or evangelize a native on some foreign mission field. All work is judged by God, and the manner and attitude with which we work can please or dishonor our Lord.

As we carry out our responsibilities on our jobs, here are some questions we would do well to ask ourselves:

- Do I regularly thank God for my job—whether it is as a president of a Fortune 500 company or as a garbage collector?

- Do I properly respect those at work in authority over me, even those whose religious, political or moral convictions are different from mine?

- Do I work heartily in whatever vocation I am placed—knowing that my service is to the Lord?

- Do I work hard even when the boss is not watching?

- Do I strive to have as good a reputation with my coworkers as I have with my fellow church members?

- Do I work as efficiently as possible so as to make my company profitable?

- Do I refrain from cutting any moral corners on the job?

- Do I make suggestions on how to improve job performance and morale?

- Do I refrain from conversations in which the boss or supervisor is criticized?

- Do I refrain from taking small items from my employee—paper clips, copy paper, pencils, etc.—even though "everyone else does it?"

- Do I make personal copies on the company copier?

- Do I use the company's Internet connection for my personal use?

- Do I fudge on my expense account or time card?

- Am I the same person on the job as I am when away from the job?

- Do I encourage employer respect, rather than helping create employee dissatisfaction?

- Are my work habits sloppy, or do I attempt to always produce work of excellence?

- Am I on time, or am I often tardy at work?

- Do I misuse sick leave or personal leave days?

- Do I abuse workers' compensation benefits?

- Do I use company time to witness to my lost co-workers, or do I wait until break time or lunch time?

- Do I remind myself regularly that my job performance and general attitude can bring either glory, or dishonor, to my Lord?

Our work does matter to God! Normally the majority of our waking hours are spent at our jobs. And how we conduct ourselves is vitally important to the cause of Christ, whether we serve as a seamstress in a factory, a politician, a preacher, a homemaker, an engineer a janitor or serve in any other area. All work should be viewed as a gift from God and as a venue of responsibility to Him. It pleases Him when we:

- Thank Him for the ability to work

- Work with all of our might

- Work as efficiently as possible

- Exhibit absolute honesty and reliability

- Realize that we are witnessing by our attitude and job performance

- Honor our bosses

- Respect our co-workers

- Pray for those with whom we work

- Set the best example we can in all respects

- Seek legitimate times and ways that we can verbally witness to those with whom we work

- Trust God, even during those times when our jobs can put us in very difficult circumstances

If you have not been practicing those things listed above, it is not too late to begin now. God is a God of second, third and fourth chances with His children. Your attitude about your job can make a world of difference to you, your family, your co-workers, your boss and ultimately will affect your relationship with the Lord.

Application

For Individuals:

1. Ask yourself and answer this question: Have I depreciated my job, thinking that since it was a "secular" job, my responsibilities were less in importance than my service at church?

2. In what ways do you need to improve your attitude and performance at work?

3. Are there supervisors, or fellow workers on the job who are lost? If so, list their names below and ask God to help you figure out a proper method, time and place for you to take the gospel to them.

For Groups:

1. Discuss some of the most common wrong attitudes we can have regarding our jobs.

2. If the boss asks us to do something about which we have questions as to whether it is morally right or wrong, what should we do?

3. If the boss asks us to do something that does not involve a moral issue, but we know that it will not be good for the company, what should we do?

4. What are some creative ways we can use to witness to lost co-workers?

Meditation

Prayerfully think through the meaning and implications of 1 Peter 2:13–25.

PUNCTUALITY
A MATTER OF OUR BEING
CONSIDERATE

"Do nothing out of selfish ambition or vain conceit, but in humility consider others better than yourselves. Each of you should look not only to your own interests, but also to the interest of others" (Philippians 2:3–4).

Christians must be considerate people. We must always be about the task of looking out for the interests of others, not those of our own. Yet many believers do not practice this when they are habitually late for church services, classes, teaching assignments, nursery work and other membership obligations.

When one commits himself to a church he is committing to attend the services. He knows when those services begin. By implication he is saying that he will be there to attend those church gatherings (not just the last forty-five minutes)! And when he says that he will teach, for example, a children's class at 9:30 AM, he is saying that he will be there at that time (or preferably earlier) and not that he will drag in five or ten minutes late, being inconsiderate of others.

And yet, sadly, there are members who are habitually late for almost every activity or responsibility. I have heard almost every imaginable excuse. In some cases they may be legitimate, but often the excuses are flimsy, many times without any foundation.

Probably the most often used alibi is "the children" or "my wife was running late." In many of these situations the real reason is that the father, who is supposed to be the spiritual leader and who is to lead the family (largely by his example) is himself the culprit. In many cases the father fails to lend any help to the mother who is trying to take care of all of the Sunday morning chores. She has to cook breakfast, get the kids up, see that they are dressed, fed and have located their Bibles and Sunday School materials. The husband often sits around reading the Sunday morning sports page without helping his harried wife. He realizes that they are now late and, on the way to church, points out that they are always late.

The above scenario does not occur in all Christian homes but, in my experience counseling families, it occurs all too frequently.

Let's think for a moment about the damage done by church members who are habitually late.

- It creates a poor atmosphere on Sundays for the entire family as one or more of the adults is frantically yelling for the other to get ready and into the car.

- Often the family arrives for a time of worship with unsettled anger between them (no way to come before the Lord).

- A very poor example is being set before the family. Children often follow in the same pattern as their parents.

- Those who keep filing in late can seriously disrupt those who have planned the services or who are teaching the class. Often their train of thought or the form of the service is interrupted.

- By arriving late, they are a distraction to others in the classes or congregation.

- When one arrives late he often misses an important ingredient which would have helped him in his understanding or Christian walk.

How does one break such a pattern of habitual lateness? We must first realize that his repeated lateness is inconsiderate of others. Next, he should begin a pattern of arriving early, not just on time. In doing so, being late because of minor delays can be eliminated. If you have left too much of the preparation to your spouse, take on a fair portion of the responsibilities for yourself. And finally, think about punctuality as a way of setting a good example for others to follow.

Application

For Individuals:

1. Are you on time (or early) to church functions?

2. What specific steps can you take to ensure that your family meets its obligation to be on time?

3. How can you assist your spouse on Sunday mornings to help your family arrive at church on time?

4. Are you teaching your children the importance of taking care of their other commitments on time?

For Groups:

1. Discuss your own experience with the group regarding punctuality. What causes people to be late?

2. Are there members of your church who habitually arrive late? Should you talk to them? If so, how should you go about it?

3. Should your pastor or church leaders address the matter of punctuality from the pulpit?

4. Other than those given above, what are some of the results of not being on time for church activities?

Meditation

Prayerfully think through the meaning and implications of 1 Corinthians 14:33.

BUILDING A PRIVATE LIBRARY

"When you come, bring the cloak that I left with Carpus at Troas and my scrolls, especially the parchments" (2 Timothy 4:13).

These words from the apostle Paul are among the last ones he wrote just prior to his death. Paul has been arrested and once again taken back to prison in Rome. He is probably now in a cold, damp cell, all alone, awaiting his execution. Most of his companions have left him and he is writing one last letter to Timothy, his faithful son in the faith. Paul is not complaining, but expressing some needs. He needs the cloak that he left in Troas (where he was probably suddenly arrested), his scrolls and especially the parchments. Some speculate that perhaps it was a warmer climate when he was arrested and he intentionally left his heavy, outer garment with Carpus. Or, that because of his sudden arrest, he did not have time to get this garment, nor did he have time to grab the scrolls and the parchments. Instead, without prior notice, he was arrested and sent to Rome, having to leave behind these valuable items.

The *parchments* were possibly his own unfinished writings, but more likely, parts of the Old Testament. The scrolls were possibly the other books he was currently using. John Gill, in his commentary on this passage, says "the apostle was a great reader of books, of various sorts, both Gentile and Jewish as appears by his citations out of the Heathen poets and his acquaintance with Jewish records, Acts 27:28; 1 Corinthians 15:33; Titus 1:1, 12; 2 Timothy 3:8."[1]

It thus appears that the apostle Paul had a few books which he took along with him on his missionary journeys. Today, pastors have ample opportunity to have good libraries, either in bound form or on the computer. Each church should encourage its pastors to use good books. Book allowances from the church can encourage this.

---

[1] John Gill, *An Exposition of the New Testament*, Vol. IX (Streamwood, IL: Primitive Baptist Library, Reprint, 1976), 543.

Books are the tools of their trade and they will need the sharpest tools available to help them in their study and preaching of the one book, the Bible. It is also extremely helpful if each church has a good library to be used by the members.

But pastors and churches are not the only ones who need libraries. Individual Christian families should have some of these tools in their homes. It would be very helpful if each church family had a library of basic Bible tools. Listed below are some books which can help form that basic library.

1. Translations and paraphrases of the Scriptures. Several of each would be helpful:

    The New American Standard Version

    The New King James Version

    English Standard Version

    The New International Version (1973, 1978 and 1984 edition)

    New Revised Standard Version

    New English Version

    The Amplified Bible

    J. B. Phillip's Translation

    King James Version

(To assist you in assessing the various Bible versions, consult Philip W. Comfort, *Essential Guide to Bible Versions*; Leland Ryken, *The Word of God in English: Criteria for Excellence in Bible Translation*; Robert L. Thomas, *How to Choose A Bible Version: Making Sense of the Proliferation of Bible Translations*.)

2. Study Bibles, such as:

    The NIV Study Bible

    The MacArthur Study Bible

    Life Application Bible

    The Spirit of the Reformation Study Bible

    The Reformation Study Bible

3. A complete concordance, such as:

    The Exhaustive Concordance of The Bible, J. Strong

    Complete Concordance to the Old and New Testaments, A. Crudens

    Analytical Concordance to the Holy Bible, R. Young

    The NIV Complete Concordance, E. W. Goodrick & John R. Kohlenberger, III

4. A Bible encyclopedia, such as:

    Zondervan's Pictorial Bible Encyclopedia (5 volumes), Merrill C. Tenney, General Editor

    International Standard Bible Encyclopedia (4 volumes), Geoffrey W. Bromiley, General Editor

5. A Bible dictionary, such as:

    The New Bible Dictionary, J. D. Douglas, Org. Ed., with F. F. Bruce, R. V. G. Tasker, J. I. Packer and D. J. Wiseman

6. Hebrew and Greek Word studies, such as:

    Vine's Expository Dictionary of New Testament Words, W. E. Vine

7. A Bible handbook, such as:

    Halley's Bible Handbook, Henry H. Halley

8. A survey of the books of the Bible:

    Bruce Wilkinson and Kenneth Boa's two volumes,

    Talk Thru the Old Testament
    Talk Thru the New Testament

9. A one-volume commentary on the Bible:

    The New Bible Commentary, F. Davidson and A. M. Stibbs and E. F. Kevan

10. A multi-volume commentary on the entire Bible:
    Matthew Henry's Commentary on the Whole Bible (6 volumes)
    Matthew Poole's Bible Commentary (3 volumes)

11. Reference work on the development of the Christian Church:
    The New International Dictionary of the Christian Church,
        J. D. Douglas, Gen. Ed.

12. A book dealing with cults and other religions:
    Dictionary of Cults, Sects, Religions and the Occult, George A.
        Mather and Larry A. Nichols

13. Biographies on outstanding Christian leaders of the past: For
    example, those on: Martin Luther, John Calvin, Charles Spur-
    geon, Adoniram Judson, John Bunyan, John Patton, David
    Livingston, etc. The life and ministry of many of these men
    can now be found on very helpful videos and DVDs.

14. A very readable systematic theology:
    Systematic Theology, Wayne Grudem

15. Christian classics:
    Pilgrim's Progress, John Bunyan (choose a modern version)
    Foxe's Book of Martyrs, John Foxe

16. Some individual books on the Christian life:
    Knowing God, J. I. Packer
    Spiritual Disciplines for the Christian Life, Donald S.
        Whitney
    The Pursuit of Holiness, Jerry Bridges
    Trusting God, Jerry Bridges

17. Books dealing with the family:
    The Christian Husband, Bob Lepine
    Exemplary Husband, Stuart Scott
    The Excellent Wife, Martha Peace
    Shepherding a Child's Heart, Tedd Tripp

18. Books on effective witnessing:

    Tell the Truth, Will Metzger

    Life Style Evangelism, Joseph Aldridge

19. Books dealing with the characters of the Bible:

    Bible Characters from the Old Testament and the New Testament, Alexander Whyte

    Personalities Around Paul, D. Edmond Hiebert

20. Books dealing with evidences, alleged errors or difficulties in the Bible:

    Evidence that Demands A Verdict, Josh McDowell

    More Evidence that Demands a Verdict, Josh McDowell

    More Than a Carpenter, Josh McDowell

    Answers to Questions, F. F. Bruce

    Hard Sayings of the Bible, Walter C. Kaiser, Jr; Peter H. Davids; F. F. Bruce; and Manfred T. Brauch

21. Catechism and Helps with Scripture Memory:

    Truth and Grace Memory Workbooks, edited by Tom Ascol. Recently published by Founders Press, this 3 volume set includes age appropriate catechism questions, Scripture memory and hymns.

22. Bible Software Programs: For today's student, there are many Bible software programs which can be purchased or can be downloaded onto a computer free of charge. These programs will include translations of Scripture, word studies, encyclopedias, commentaries, maps, surveys, and other study tools. Hundreds of such helps can be located by simply inserting "Bible Software" into your search engine. The costs vary. Some are free to download while others cost from a few dollars to several hundreds of dollars to purchase. You can also enter a biblical word or name, a theological subject, the name of a writer, or other concept dealing with the Scriptures into your search engine and you will be amazed at the number of helps right

at your fingertips. These are wonderful ways to save both time and expense in your study of the Word of God.

There are many more superb books which could be added to this list. That makes it hard to leave any out and so it is very tempting to try to list them all. But my purpose is to encourage each family to have at least a few good, basic tools at hand. The entire list mentioned above could probably be purchased for somewhere around $1,000, especially if a discount book service was used. If a family could not afford this amount at one time, perhaps books could be added every few months, or they could serve as birthday or Christmas presents until a basic library is built. These books will last for a lifetime and will be a valuable aid in helping to understand God's Word. Keep in mind, though, that writers can be mistaken in some areas. So always read with a certain amount of caution. The Bible, alone, is the only infallible book.

Application

For Individuals:

1. Make a list of your current basic library tools. Are there any of these books which you should add to your list at this time?

2. Determine how much money you could set aside over the next year to build up your family library.

3. If needed, talk to your church leaders about specific titles they recommend.

4. Purchase some of the low-cost evangelistic books listed below which you could keep on hand to give to the lost. Here are two which have, for a number of years, proven their worth worldwide: *Ultimate Questions* and *Right With God*, both by John Blanchard. Recently Jim Elliff has written an excellent evangelistic tool, *Pursuing God: A Seeker's Guide.* This 69 page booklet is attractive, clear, interestingly written and presents the basics of the gospel in a compelling fashion. It may be ordered from Christian Communicators Worldwide, 201 Main, Suite #3, Parkville, MO 64152 USA.

For Groups:

1. Discuss the basic books (their title, author, style and purpose) that you have found helpful in your study of God's Word.

2. If your church does not have a good lending library, what can you do to help the church to establish one?

3. Do your pastors have good libraries? If not, what can your group do to help them to obtain additional study tools?

Meditation

Prayerfully think through the meaning and implications of 1 Timothy 4:11–16.

PERSEVERANCE
KEEP ON KEEPING ON!

"We always thank God for all of you, mentioning you in our prayers. We continually remember before our God and Father your work produced by faith, your labor prompted by love, and your **endurance** inspired by hope in our Lord Jesus Christ" (1 Thessalonians 1:3). Therefore, among God's churches we boast about your **perseverance** and faith in all the persecutions and trials you are **enduring**" (2 Thessalonians 1:4).

Christian perseverance and preservation are two sides of an important biblical truth. The Scriptures teach that God will wonderfully preserve those who have genuine faith in the Lord Jesus Christ. He tells us that we are saved eternally, not temporarily (John 3:16). He promises us that He will never leave us nor forsake us (Hebrews13:5). He tells us that He will definitely raise up all those who come by faith to His Son (John 6:39–40). He tells us that we are kept in the Father's hands and that nothing can take us out of the Father's hands (John 10.29). He says that nothing in all creation shall separate us from His love (Romans 8:39).

And yet there is another side to that truth. We must continue in the faith (Acts 14:22; Colossians 1:23; 1 Timothy 2:15). We must strive and hold out to the end (2 Peter 1:5–11). We must *persevere* (Ephesians 6:10–18; James 1:12). God's *preservation* of all of His saints and the saints' *perseverance* are two biblical truths which we would call an antinomy. To our minds they may appear contradictory, yet in God's inscrutable plan they are both equally true. We must *persevere* to the end and at the same time we know that God will *preserve* all those who are truly His.

In the two verses quoted above, Paul writes about the Thessalonians' perseverance. They were enduring in their commitment to the Lord despite serious persecution and trials. It is interesting that Paul commends them this way in the early verses of both of his letters to them. Paul, of course, had helped establish the church in Thessalonica and was later forbidden to return to the city. Most commentators think that the bond that Jason (a member of the church) was required to post, in a direct or indirect way, probably had affected Paul's freedom to re-visit the church. Paul had to be content to get his information about the Thessalonians through Timothy who remained behind in Thessalonica. Yet Paul was very close to this church's members and in his first letter he talked about serving both as a father and a mother to them. The word that he received through Timothy was heart-warming because he learned that they were persevering in the work of the gospel.

When we think about perseverance, our minds often jump to the Holy Spirit's inner work in our lives enabling us to hang on to the faith. However, perseverance should also be thought of in the context of the members of a local church working together and persevering in their service, love and devotion to each other. In the Philippian letter Paul prays that their "love would abound more and more" and that they may "grow in their understanding of what is best and may be pure and blameless *until the day of Christ Jesus*" (1:9–10). Later in the letter Paul urges them to "*continue to work out their salvation with fear and trembling*" (2:12). While these verses definitely envision the Spirit's work in these individual Christians, the statements are in the immediate context of the local church in Philippi. Paul addresses these church members about their responsibility to each other in the local congregation.

The writer of Hebrews gives an interesting command in chapter 3, verses 12–13: "See to it brothers, that none of you has a sinful, unbelieving heart that turns away from the living God. But encourage *one another* daily, as long as it is called today, so that none of you may be hardened by sin's deceitfulness." The writer places the responsibility on each of us to *each other* to see that none fall away (that all *persevere*). Normally we think of this as the Spirit of God's work, coupled with the individuals' responsibility to hold out faithfully to the end. Yet here in Hebrews, the writer charges all members of the Christian community with the responsibility of seeing that none "has a sinful, unbelieving heart that turns away from the living God." Therefore, my brother's perseverance is partly my obligation.

Certainly the prime responsibility rests with him and the power to persevere comes from the sovereign Spirit, yet I must play a role in his perseverance.

When this truth is understood it opens up for us many additional avenues of service within our local church. If a fellow member begins to stray away, I must go after him. When one falls into sin, I must try to restore him. When one is weak or troubled, I am to be there to help restore his joy in the Lord. When one is shirking his duties before the Lord, I am to patiently challenge him before our God. He is not an island off to himself. Neither am I. I have responsibilities to *each member* of the body. While I must keep on, keeping on, I must also help my brother or sister to keep on, keeping on.

Obviously, one of the best ways I can help my fellow-members persevere is to pray for them. The Holy Spirit is sovereign and more powerful than all of my efforts. But I should not stop with prayer only. I am to put shoe leather to my prayers for my brothers and sisters in the Lord.

In order to help others I, myself, must persevere in my own walk before the Lord. I should not be trying to take a splinter out of my brother's eye when I have a large beam in my own eye. I must persevere if I am to help my brother keep on, keeping on.

Here are some very practical areas that need the perseverance of the members of the local body:

- Long-term commitment to the body

- Faithful attendance at church functions

- Regular financial support of the church

- Optimistic outlook for God's blessings on the body

- A faithful witness to the lost in our community

- Deep commitment to prayer, both for the members and the leadership

- Continued service wherever needed and equipped, regardless of how unexciting

- Encouraging support of the church leadership

- Faithfully exercising both the formative and corrective discipline programs of the church

These are many other areas that could be covered. Too many members begin in a local church full of an optimistic desire to serve, but as time passes, initiatives and interest fade. Yet, God wants us to persevere, even when all those around us may be failing. Paul commended the Thessalonians for their endurance and he called on the Philippians to continue to work out their salvation (collectively). These commands are also for us today, especially in a time when personal commitment is low in both our society and in our churches.

Application

For Individuals:

1. Have you started in a service area and then dropped aside without a good reason? If so, ask the Lord to forgive you and restart your service.

2. Think through the members of your own local church. Are there members who have fallen aside? If so, list several names here and what you personally plan to do about them.

3. Briefly go through Paul's letters (Romans through Titus) and make a note of some of his commands where you are to look out after the interests of others. Then consider your personal service in light of these many admonitions.

For Groups:

1. Suggest and discuss other verses that talk about the believer's perseverance.

2. It is clear in Scripture that a true child of God will not totally fall away; yet some professing believers do so. How should we view fellow church members who do not seem to persevere in the faith, and what actions should the church take?

3. Discuss what occurs in a church when professing believers turn aside and no longer walk in obedience to Christ.

Meditation

Prayerfully think through the meaning and implications of
2 Peter 1:5–11.

Section Two

Joining a Body

THE CHURCH
UNIVERSAL & LOCAL

The Universal Church: "... and on this rock I will build my church" (Matthew 16:18); "... because I persecuted the church of God" (1 Corinthians 15:9); "... just as Christ loved the church... to present her to himself as a radiant church" (Ephesians 5:25–27); "... for the sake of his body, which is the church" (Colossians 1:24); "to the church of the firstborn, whose names are written in heaven" (Hebrews 12:23).

The Local Church: "If he refuses to listen to them, tell it to the church" (Matthew 18:17); "In the church at Antioch there were prophets and teachers" (Acts 13:1); "From Miletus, Paul sent to Ephesus for the elders of the church" (Acts 20:13); "I commend to you our sister, Phoebe, a servant of the church in Cenchreae" (Romans 16:1); "Greet also the church that meets at their house" (Romans 16:5); "To the angel of the church in Ephesus, write" (Revelation 2:1).

It is clear from the Scripture references above that the New Testament speaks of both the *church universal* (which comprises all of the true believers throughout history, from every kindred, tribe and tongue) and also speaks of *local churches* (which consist of all of those separate bodies of Christ who meet together for worship, study, prayer and communion, in local congregations).

The *Universal Church* has in it only true believers, ones who have been called by the Spirit to trust in the saving work of Christ, who are kept eternally by the love of God and who will be presented to Christ without spot or blemish.

Local Churches have in their membership people who are professing believers, some of whom are genuinely saved, while others are unsaved and are still lost in their sins. Sometimes it is impossible to clearly distinguish between the two, because often unbelieving members exhibit many of the outward characteristics of believers. But the Lord knows who are His.

By far most of the commands in the New Testament are given to believers in the context of local churches. Christians (and church leaders) are told:

- To guard the flock (Acts 20:28, 31)

- To use their spiritual gifts for each other (Romans 12:3–13; 1 Corinthians 12:1–30; Ephesians 4:7–16; 1 Peter 4:7–11)

- To rejoice with those who rejoice and to mourn with those who mourn (Romans 12:15)

- For the strong and the weak brothers to accept one another (Romans 14:1–15:13)

- Not to fellowship with a brother who is living in unrepentant sin (1 Corinthians 5:1–13)

- To make judgments regarding disputes (1 Corinthians 6:1–11)

- To support those who preach and teach (1 Corinthians 9:1–27)

- To take communion together in a worthy manner (1 Corinthians 11:17–34)

- To collect a relief offering on the first day of the week (1 Corinthians 16:1–4)

- To greet one another with a holy kiss (1 Corinthians 16:19; 2 Corinthians 13:12)

- To forgive a repentant sinner (2 Corinthians 2:5–11)

- To restore a brother (Galatians 6:1)

- To carry each others' burdens (Galatians 6:2)

- To look after the interests of others (Philippians 2:4)

- To help solve member problems (Philippians 4:3)

- To keep away from those who are idle (2 Thessalonians 3:6–15)

- To choose qualified elders and deacons (1 Timothy 3:1–13; Titus 1:5-9)

- To honor spiritual leaders (1 Timothy 5:17–19)

- To warn those who are false teachers and those who are quarrelsome (2 Timothy 2:14–26)

- To teach one another (Titus 2:1–10)

- To remind the members to be obedient to authority (Titus 3:1–2)

- To warn a divisive person (Titus 3:9–11)

- To encourage one another daily (Hebrews 3:12–15)

- Not to forsake assembling themselves together in the local church (Hebrews 10:25)

- To look after orphans and widows (James 1:27)

- Not to show favoritism (James 2:1–4)

- To confess their sins to each other and to pray for each other (James 5:13–16)

- To serve as examples to the flock (1 Peter 5:1–4)

- To be submissive to elders (1 Peter 5:5)

- To repent (Revelation 2:1–3:22)

This is not a complete list, but merely a sampling of the many commands given to and for the local churches in the New Testament—and to our churches today.

There are many professing Christians who do not attend a local church, saying that they "can be a Christian without going to church." However, it is clear from the many examples given above that such people cannot be *obedient* Christians, for these commands must be obeyed in the context of a local church.

Trying to be a "lone ranger" Christian, outside of a church body, causes one to also miss the many joys one can have in the local church, such as fellowshipping with brothers and sisters of like mind, rejoicing with those who rejoice, jointly promoting the gospel, caring for each other spiritually, physically and financially, praying for each other, restoring one another, even weeping with those who weep. To cut ourselves off from these wonderful opportunities is to rob ourselves of many of the blessings Christ provided for us through the *local church*. It is also to disobey the Head of the church. Church involvement should be He–centered rather than me–centered.

Application

For Individuals:

1. Are you a member of a local church? What are some ways in which you have been blessed through your local church?

2. What are some of the protections you receive as a member of a local church?

3. Are you an active member, or are you on the sidelines? If the latter, for what reasons? What would Christ have you doing?

For Groups:

1. Discuss other New Testament commands given to the local church.

2. What are some of the excuses which people give for not becoming active members in a local body?

3. What are some of the bad things which can happen to those professing Christians who refuse to participate in a local church?

Meditation

Prayerfully think through the meaning and implications of Matthew 16:18 and 18:17.

JUST HOW IMPORTANT IS
THE CHURCH?

"… I am writing you these instructions so that, if I am de-
layed, you will know how people ought to conduct themselves
in God's household, which is the church of the living God,
the pillar and foundation of the truth" (1 Timothy 3:14–15).

I became a Christian in the spring of my senior year in high
school. That fall I went away to college and worked part-time in an
insurance office to pay for my college education. Though it was difficult to both work and take a full college load, I was nevertheless
excited about my new life in Christ. I was going to church regularly,
studying the Bible daily, reading good books, meeting new Christian
friends, learning to pray and growing in Christ. Those were very joyful and exciting times.

Toward the end of my freshman year I realized I was going to
need more money than the seventy-five cents per hour I was making
on my job (that was in 1955). I heard of a job on a large company
farm near Chicago where college boys could make good money. So
I loaded my belongings in a small black trunk, boarded a train and
headed to Mendota, Illinois, really not knowing for sure what I was
getting into. Shortly after my arrival, the canning company for which
I worked, assigned me and several other young men from across the
nation to a pea farm, where they housed us in some rather plain
barracks, fed us three meals a day and worked us seven days a week,
often as much as sixteen to twenty hours per day. It was hard, dirty,
dangerous work, but where else in 1955 could a college student earn
up to $200 per week, with no living expenses?

When we began that summer there were a few believers among
the crew and we had some rich fellowship on that farm. But soon
the hard work, long hours and homesickness began to take their toll.
Serious attrition began. Within a few weeks I was the only college
student left on that particular farm. In order to complete the crops

that summer, the company began to pick up men off skid row in Chicago and bring them to live and work on the farm. The result was that I was the only Christian there, with no one else left to provide me with spiritual fellowship. Many of the men were alcoholics and were foul-mouthed derelicts. Thus began some very lonesome days. I was starving for spiritual conversation. Yet I needed the money if I hoped to return to college that fall.

Finally, late in the summer we received a Sunday off in order to rest. That morning I hitched a ride into town and made my way to a small, white frame building, which housed the local Baptist church. But much to my dismay a sign was stapled to the door, which read: "Closed for the summer."

The remainder of my time there that summer was spent with no Christian fellowship. My only spiritual stimulation was my Bible and the few Christian books I had with me.

I now believe that this episode in my life was used by God to show me the vital importance of the local church. All one has to do to recognize this is to be without one. I am glad the Lord taught me this lesson early in my Christian life. Several times later while on mission trips, the need of a local church was made much clearer to me. In some of those areas of the world, there have been many villages where there were no Christian churches whatsoever. My heart bled for those individual believers who were forced to live and grow spiritually all on their own.

In America, particularly in the southern Bible belt, we are very spoiled. Churches abound. In some of these areas churches are on almost every corner. This is not true in many parts of the globe. To be without a local family of God is to miss some of God's richest blessings. Just how important is your church? Consider the following:

- It provides you with daily and weekly fellowship.

- It warns and encourages you.

- It helps hold you accountable.

- It provides communion for you.

- It challenges you to use your spiritual gifts.

- It provides a place for those gifts to be exercised.

- It helps protect you from heresy.

- It guides you to godly living.

- It spiritually ministers to your family.

- It collectively supports Christian causes and missions around the world.

- It often means the salvation of souls (perhaps even your own).

- It helps you when you are spiritually, emotionally, physically or financially in need.

- It is the pillar and ground of the truth in your area.

- It disciplines you when you develop a sinful lifestyle.

- It helps bring down racial barriers.

These are just a few of the benefits of belonging to a good local church. Try to imagine where else you could receive such benefits and direction. Indeed, our Lord manifested His wisdom when He established both the universal and the local bodies of Christ. And we are the primary beneficiaries. Today, thank God for the grace shown to you in placing you in a sound, local church body. If you are not in one, either find one to join, or help start an evangelical church in your area. It will be an important key to your spiritual growth and service.

Application

For Individuals:

1. Have you thanked God for His wisdom and grace in placing you in a good church?

2. Have you lately encouraged others to be grateful for your local congregation?

3. What specific things can you be doing to help your church do a better job of meeting the needs of the members? The needs of the community? The needs of the universal church? And finally, the needs of the world at large?

For Groups:

1. Discuss what life would be like for Christians if Christ had not established local churches.

2. Talk about the basic ingredients which are needed for any group of Christians to legitimately be called a church.

3. Talk about the churches in Revelation 2 and 3. Why was Christ unhappy with them and what about them pleased Him?

Meditation

Prayerfully think through the meaning and implications of 1 Corinthians 12:1–30.

JOINING A CHURCH

"Every day they continued to meet together in the temple courts. ... And the Lord added to their number daily those who were being saved" (Acts 2:46–47a).

There are Christians who will not formally join a church because they do not see explicit verses in the New Testament which speaks of a "membership roll." These people will attend a church regularly, will support the church with their prayers, give of their finances and personal commitment, but will not formally join the church. For them it seems wrong to ask people to do something which the New Testament does not explicitly teach.

Others have a strong view of the universal body of Christ and believe that since they are a part of that body of believers from all around the globe, attendance in a local congregation is not necessary.

Others do not see the universal body of Christ taught in the Bible and for them the only emphasis in the New Testament is the local church.

Finally, there are those who believe in both the universal and the local church but who, for various reasons, do not want to be committed to a local congregation. They often say, "I can be a Christian without going to church." Perhaps they have been offended by a church member or are in disagreement with some church activity, or want to keep their Sundays for themselves. Whatever the reason, they have decided that they can serve Christ without a commitment to a local church body.

It is true that you will look in vain in the New Testament to find specific mention of a membership list. However, you can find many references to our responsibilities within the context of a local church. See, for example, Matthew 18:15–18; Acts 20:28–29; 1 Corinthians 5:1–8; 11:17–34; 12:27–31; 14:22–40; 2 Corinthians 2:5–11; Ephesians 4:11–16; Philippians 2:25–30; 4:14–19; 2 Thessalonians 3:6–15; 1 Timothy 2:1–15; 3:1–16; 5:1–22; Titus 1:5–2:10; James 5:13–16; 1 Peter 5:1–5.

You will also find references to the local body itself: Acts 11:22; 13:1; 14:27; 15:12, 22, 30; 20:17; Romans 16:1, 5, 23; 1 Corinthians 1:2; 4:17; 11:18; Colossians 4:15; 1 Thessalonians 1:1; Philemon 2.

In the New Testament era (the first century) there seems to have been only one church in each locality, though parts of that local body probably met in different locations. Today the situation is vastly different. In many areas there are churches within a few blocks of each other. And so, today, we have ample opportunity to join congregations of our own choosing.

How, then, should we go about selecting a church for our family and ourselves? How can we be sufficiently informed about the church to which we are committing ourselves? This is a very important issue and it is critical that we make a proper assessment before we make such a commitment. Here are some suggestions:

- As a visitor, attend all of the services: Worship hours, Sunday school, Sunday night services, mid-week activities, home cell groups, weekly Bible studies.

- Ask for and read carefully the doctrinal statement, church constitution and bylaws, history of the church, missions program, church mission statement, financial reports, leadership structure.

- Meet with the pastors. Ask them about their theological views as well as their ministry plans and methods.

- Learn about the children's ministry. Ask specific questions about the nursery, children's classes and activities, the curriculum being used and the youth activities.

- Find out what ministry areas and opportunities are available in which you could serve.

- Ask about the type of sermons most often preached, whether they are primarily expository, topical, textual, biographical, etc. Ask who does the majority of the preaching and if there is any rotation among the staff. Seek to know if you could grow spiritually in that environment.

- Ask for information about their benevolence program and any other ministries to the poor and/or inner city.

- Make sure that all races are openly welcomed and that individuals of various socio-economic levels will be comfortable.

- Determine if the church has a healthy spread of all ages.

- Ask about their worship style. Is it traditional, contemporary, or a mixture of both? Determine if their style is an issue for you.

- Inquire about whether the congregation is one characterized by peace among members, or if there are serious factions, which might result in a church split.

- Ask about the longevity of each pastor.

- Ask the leadership what their leadership style is and to what form of shepherding of the flock they are committed.

- Find out if the church is solvent, or is heavily in debt.

- If possible, spend some time with a cross-section of the members. Get to know them and determine how compatible you would be with them.

- Try to find out if they have a full-orbed ministry (to children, youth, singles, adults, elderly, shut-ins, the poor, missions, etc.).

- Ask if the church practices church discipline and if so, what form it takes.

- Determine if true Christian fellowship is emphasized among the members.

- Seek to determine if you are really needed in that particular body and if your gifts would be called upon, or is there another evangelical church in that vicinity which might be in serious need of your special gifts and talents.

These are just a few of the things that you should look into and seriously consider before you join a congregation. Keep in mind that you are not going to find complete satisfaction in all of these areas. There is no such thing as a perfect church. And if you strain at all of the minor issues you may never locate a church that would be acceptable to you. But determine what the critical areas are and make your decision based on those matters.

There should be some non-negotiables on which you must never compromise. In particular, make certain that the church is committed to:

- The Bible as the fully inspired, inerrant, infallible and authoritative Word of God.

- That God is exalted as holy, sovereign and all-wise.

- That salvation is by grace alone, through faith alone, in Christ alone.

- That there is solid, biblical, expository preaching and teaching.

- That the church recognizes its duty to evangelize its own community and those around the world through missionary efforts.

- That it teaches and insists upon holiness among its membership.

- That it encourages the proper use of God-given gifts within the body.

- That it is characterized by a love toward both the saved and the lost.

- That it both feeds and protects the flock.

- That it encourages genuine fellowship among its members.

- That it is a church that prays, recognizing its absolute dependence upon the grace of God.

- That it is a vibrant, joyful Christian fellowship.

Once you are satisfied with your assessment that the church is committed to these things, commit yourself to that congregation and serve there with all of your heart.

Application

For Individuals:

1. Are you currently a member of a local body?

2. If not, what steps are you taking to locate one?

3. If you cannot find a sound local congregation in your area, what could you be doing to help form a church where the truth is taught?

For Groups:

1. Discuss what you think are the essentials required of a church in order for you to join it.

2. Is it wrong to permanently attend a church without ever joining it?

3. If you were to help establish a church, or were to help establish a mission from your church, what steps would you include to aid them in becoming a church with which Christ would be pleased?

Meditation

Prayerfully think through the meaning and implications of Ephesians 4:11–16.

BAPTISM
ITS SUBJECTS AND MODE

"The eunuch asked Philip, 'Tell me, please, who is the prophet talking about, himself or someone else?' Then Philip began with that very passage of Scripture and told him the good news about Jesus. As they traveled along the road, they came to some water and the eunuch said, 'Look, here is water. Why shouldn't I be baptized?' And he ordered the chariot to stop. Then both Philip and the eunuch went down into the water and Philip baptized him. When they came up out of the water, the Spirit of the Lord suddenly took Philip away, and the eunuch did not see him again, but went on his way rejoicing" (Acts 8:34–39).

In this passage we discover several aspects of baptism. For example, a brand new disciple of Christ is immediately baptized upon his coming to faith in Christ. We have in this example the proper mode of baptism: immersion (they "went down into the water... and...came up out of the water" (vss. 38 and 39).

There are, of course, others who hold different views on baptism. Many Catholics, some Churches of Christ and others believe baptism is necessary for salvation or is the cause of regeneration. These views are heretical and should be vigorously opposed.

For a good discussion of the various views on baptism from a Baptistic perspective see Wayne Grudem, *Systematic Theology* (Grand Rapids: Zondervan, 1994), 966–987, and from a Reformed or Presbyterian perspective see Louis Berkhof, *Systematic Theology*, (Grand Rapids: Eerdmans, 1996), 622–643. While the differences in these two points of view are significant, they should not eliminate fellowship between genuine Christian believers. These differences do not involve the basic gospel truths, such as the inspiration and authority of the Scriptures, the divinity of Christ, the sacrificial work of Christ, salvation by grace alone, through faith alone in Christ alone and other essential teachings.

This study is written from the perspective that baptism should be administered only to individuals who give a credible testimony of conversion and that the proper mode of baptism is immersion. From this perspective, here are some principles from the Word of God.

- Baptism is clearly a command of Christ; it is not an option (Matthew 28:19).

- Baptism and the Lord's Supper are the two ordinances ordained by Christ (Matthew 28:19; 26:26–29; 1 Corinthians 11:23–25).

- The basic meaning of the term "baptism" is to "plunge, dip, or immerse" (See Grudem, p. 967, mentioned above).

- Immersion is the picture one gets when looking at the baptisms in the New Testament (Mark 1:5; 1:10; John 3:23; Acts 8:36–39).

- Baptism symbolizes our union with Christ in His death, burial and resurrection (Romans 6:3–4; Colossians 2:12).

- Baptism is a visual commitment to put off our old way of life and a pledge that we will walk in the newness of the Spirit (Romans 6:1–14).

- The only subjects of baptism are genuine believers (Acts 2:41; 8:12; 10:47–48).

- Baptism in no way saves a person. Faith alone saves (Romans 1:16–17; 3:28; Ephesians 2:8–9).

- In the New Testament, baptism immediately followed conversion (Acts 2:41; 8:38; 16:33).

- In the household baptisms in the New Testament, those who were baptized were those who had joyfully embraced the gospel (Acts 2:39, compare the first part of the verse with the last part of the verse; Acts 8:12–13; compare Acts 16:33 with verses 32 and 34; compare 1 Corinthians 1:16 with verse 16:15).

- Though it seems best that baptism should be administered in the context of a local church, individuals may perform baptism (Acts 8:38).

Many other points can be made regarding this important subject, for there has been much written to explain and defend the various positions. It is sad to know that genuine Christians have sometimes divided themselves from the fellowship of other believers over this subject. The purpose here is not to cause harmful division but to stress the importance and joy of baptism. It is a wonderful symbolic picture of our having died and been buried with Christ, and of our resurrection with Christ. It presents a soul which has been eternally saved and a life which is being transformed by the gospel. And it is an excellent opportunity to share one's new faith with those who witness the baptismal service.

Application

For Individuals:

1. Have you been properly baptized as a believer?

2. Baptism is just one way, though an important way, of telling others about the changes in your life. In what other ways do you plan to express these changes to others?

3. As you witness to others, perhaps you will have the joyful privilege of seeing some of those people express their new life in Christ by their own baptism. Make a list of people to whom you should witness over the next year.

For Groups:

1. Read and discuss the passages mentioned above with regard to both the subjects and mode of baptism.

2. Discuss some wrong assumptions and mistakes made concerning baptism.

3. Does your church properly administer baptism? If not, how can you help effect change in your church? How could your church improve the baptismal services?

Meditation

Prayerfully think through the meaning and implications of 1 Corinthians 1:13-17.

THE LORD'S SUPPER
ITS MEANING AND OBSERVANCE

"While they were eating, Jesus took bread, gave thanks and broke it, and gave it to his disciples, saying, 'Take and eat; this is my body.' Then he took the cup, gave thanks and offered it to them, saying, 'Drink from it, all of you. This is my blood of the covenant, which is poured out for many for the forgiveness of sins. I tell you, I will not drink from this fruit of the vine from now on until that day when I drink it anew with you in my Father's kingdom'" (Matthew 26:26–29).

This wonderful ordinance established by Christ Himself had its roots in the Old Testament in the Messianic types and shadows such as the sacrifices and the Passover meal. In the New Testament it is presented as a beautiful symbol of the broken body and shed blood of our Lord and Savior. The observance is also spoken of as "communion" or in some circles, "the Eucharist."

Regarding the Lord's Supper, Catholics hold to a position known as "transubstantiation." According to their view when the priest who is holding up the bread and wine declares, "This is my body," then the bread and wine actually become the body and blood of Christ.

Lutherans hold to a position known as "consubstantiation." According to this position the physical body of Christ is present "in, with, and under" the bread of the Lord's Supper. Though Christ's body is not visible, yet they consider it to be there by the Word of God.

Other Christians maintain that the Lord's Supper is symbolic and is done in remembrance of the Lord. Important things take place when believers observe this ordinance:

- It is a vivid reminder of Christ's broken body and shed blood (Matthew 26:26–28; 1 Corinthians. 11:23–27).

- We meditate on Christ's death on our behalf (Matthew 26:28; 1 Corinthians 11:24).

- It is a time of affirmation that we are participants in Christ's sacrifice (1 Corinthians 10:16–17).

- It is a reminder that someday we will be with the risen Christ in His Father's kingdom (Matthew 26:29).

- It is a proclamation that Christ will come again (1 Corinthians 11:26).

- It brings to our minds that the New Covenant, in which all true believers participate, was established by Christ's sacrificing of His flesh and His blood. This New Covenant carries both great privileges and important responsibilities (Matthew 26:28; 1 Corinthians 11:25).

- It is a time of reflection during which participants should examine themselves to see if there are any broken relationships between them and other members of the body (1 Corinthians 11:27–28).

- It is a time of rich fellowship for the body of Christ in which we affirm that though many, we are one in Christ (1 Corinthians 10:16–17; 11:17–22).

- It includes a warning for those who participate in an unworthy manner (1 Corinthians 10:18–22; 11:29–32).

Because of the words of Scripture presented above, it is clear that only those who have been regenerated and who are personally trusting in the saving work of Christ on their behalf should participate in this observance.

The Scriptures do not tell us how often the Lord's Supper should be observed. Some churches observe it every Sunday while others do so only at monthly or quarterly intervals. What is clear is that the participants must understand the meaning of this ordinance.

The Scriptures also do not insist that we use a particular element in its observance. Some use particles of bread or crackers, some unleavened bread or whole loaves of bread, which are broken by the members. Some churches use only unfermented grape juice, while others prefer to use wine. (Some provide grape juice and wine on the same tray so that an individual member may decide for himself which to use.) The churches and their leadership have the right to offer any of these elements for this observance.

The Scriptures also do not tell us who must officiate at the observance of the Lord's Supper. Pastors/Elders, Deacons, or laymen may be selected to conduct the Lord's Supper, though in most churches the leaders (Pastors/Elders) are the ones who conduct the public services. Communion may be served to shut-ins in their homes or care facilities by any of the men mentioned to whom the privilege is delegated.

The frequency of the observance, the elements of the observance, and those who officiate at the observance are not the critical issues. What is important is that those who participate recognize the symbolic and spiritual meaning of the ordinance, and examine themselves carefully to make sure that they are participants in the actual broken body and shed blood of Christ. Coupled with that, there is to be a serious examination to assure that any broken relationships within the body of Christ are repaired before participation in this wonderful commemoration of the betrayal, death, burial, resurrection and second coming of our Lord and Savior, Jesus Christ.

Application

For Individuals:

1. Before you participate in the next communion service, make certain that Christ is your personal Savior.

2. Before you participate in the next communion service, make certain that there are no broken relationships between you and any other members of the body of Christ. If there are, attempt to repair them.

3. If you have children, carefully explain to them the true meaning of the Lord's Supper, and why they should participate only after they become true believers.

For Groups:

1. Read the passages mentioned above in Matthew and 1 Corinthians and discuss in some detail the many truths found in them.

2. In what ways have you seen the Lord's Supper observed during which your were particularly blessed?

3. Are there ways in which your church could make its present practice of the Lord's Supper more meaningful? If so, suggest those ways to your church leadership.

Meditation

Prayerfully think through the meaning and implications of 1 Corinthians 11:27–32.

Section Three

The Body at Work

THE CHURCH—A BODY

"From him the whole body, joined and held together by every supporting ligament, grows and builds itself up in love, as each part does its work... Christ is the head of the church, his body...." (Ephesians 4:16; 5:23).

The church in the New Testament is presented by several analogies, such as God's household (Ephesians 3:19), a building (Ephesians 3:21), a temple (2 Corinthians 6:15) and the pillar and ground of truth (1 Timothy 3:15). One of the best known but perhaps the least appreciated representations of the church is as a *body* (Ephesians 4:16; 4:23–32) and we as members of that body. That pictures a cohesive whole, active, living organism. Unfortunately in our times, individualism seems to have taken over our society and has also crept into our churches at an alarming rate.

Gone seem to be the days when members of local churches felt a serious obligation to the church body as a whole. Years ago the church was looked upon as one's family. If any part of the family (the body) suffered, all suffered. If any part was in need, the family came together with open hands and hearts. If any had abundance, it was shared among the family. If anyone was hurting, all hurt. When one rejoiced, all rejoiced.

When any part of our physical body hurts, our whole body sympathizes with that part. If one's foot is sore, the leg and the hip compensate for it and protect it. If any disease occurs, the immune system throughout the body gathers its forces to fight the intruder.

Furthermore, the hand does not say to the knee, "I don't like you so I am going to ignore you, or get you out of my sight." The finger does not say to the eye, "I do not like your looks so I am going to gouge you out." Nor does the foot say to the ear, "I don't really need you so I am going to walk anywhere I want to, despite the warning sound you are hearing." The throat does not say to the tastebuds, "You may be tasting something awful, but I am going to swallow whatever I want. I don't need to listen to your advice."

Unfortunately, members of the body of Christ often act in such foolish, selfish ways. God never intended it to be that way in His body. Just as He designed our physical bodies to work harmoniously together, so He has designed His church body to build each other up, love each other, listen to each other, care for each other and to protect each other.

This requires that we give up part of our individualism when we become a part of Christ's church—and especially when we join a local congregation. First and foremost, our chief concern should be the good of the body at large rather than our own personal tastes and preferences. It means that we become a part of a family of believers and that we take our family responsibilities seriously. Their interests become more important than our own (Philippians 2:3). When a disease appears (perhaps false teaching, unrepentant sins, doubts, discouragement) we bring all of our gifts, talents and resources to bear to help solve the problem.

When a brother or sister is in a financial calamity, our resources become theirs. When a member falls into some sudden serious sin, we are to patiently restore him, rather than attacking, vilifying, or disparaging him behind his back. Someone has said that Christians are the only army that shoots its wounded! When the body as a whole becomes sick or injured, we don't run off, but rather try to find the source of the malady and apply the appropriate remedy.

Bodies do not separate. I've never seen an arm or an ear just separate from the rest of the body and go join another body. Similarly, church members must recognize their responsibility to stick with their family unless radical amputation is absolutely necessary. Yet, too often today, members just walk away from each other for the slightest reason. Perhaps it was that the worship style was no longer exciting, or their feelings were hurt by some innocent, casual remark. Sometimes they think they must carry too much of the load. Or, as often is the case, another body becomes more attractive—perhaps with more dynamic preaching, a newer building, more rapid growth, or a more "exciting" worship hour.

And so, despite their earlier commitments and often without any warning, they just walk away. They do what feels good to them personally. Never mind that it hurts the remaining body terribly. What is more important is what is pleasing to them individually.

That is a far cry from Christ's concept of His church. If you want to see a picture of the church perfected, just consider what it is like in heaven. There it is a harmonious body worshipping (and working) together around the throne of Christ. And there will be no separations of any kind. No one will ever say, "I have no need of you," and simply walk away!

Application

For Individuals:

1. Do you honestly look upon yourself and other members as an important part of your local congregation?

2. If another member needs some of your time, talents, or resources, do you look upon that as an imposition, or as an opportunity to share that with which God has entrusted you?

3. What can you do for your church body this week? This month? This year?

For Groups:

1. Discuss other New Testament analogies of a local church. When all of these are put together, what does the picture of the church look like?

2. Using the image of a body, what are some of the things Christ is portraying for us regarding the church?

3. Discuss how this picture differs from what one sees in many modern churches.

Meditation

Prayerfully think about the meaning and implications of Romans 12:3–8; Ephesians 5:21–32 and Galatians 6:1–10.

VOLUNTEERISM . . . OR RESPONSIBILITY?

"Each one should use whatever spiritual gift he has received to serve others, faithfully administering God's grace in its various forms. If anyone speaks, he should do it as one speaking the very words of God. If anyone serves, he should do it with the strength God provides, so that in all things God may be praised through Jesus Christ. To him be the glory and the power for ever and ever. Amen" (1 Peter 4:10–11).

Like most churches, ours has a large team of volunteers. We have members who have volunteered to work in the nursery, to clean our building, to keep the grounds mowed, to operate the sound system, to make our tape recordings, to answer incoming phone calls, to teach our classes, to serve as Deacons, Elders and Trustees, to mention but a few. Without these "volunteers" our church could not carry out her ministry.

Yet, when we look into the Word of God, it never speaks of *volunteers.* It speaks of those who freely serve and who recognize they have a joyful *obligation to serve others* in whatever manner they are capable (or gifted). In the New Testament the four basic passages dealing with the believers' use of their gifts are Romans 12, 1 Corinthians 12, Ephesians 4 and 1 Peter 4. In these passages we learn that Christ has sovereignly distributed His gifts to His church through her various members and that they are responsible to use these gifts (interests, talents, training, resources, opportunities) to faithfully serve others.

Nowhere in Scripture do we have the slightest hint that God's people are to *volunteer.* Rather, the Scriptures indicate that the use of our gifts should be considered a joyful *responsibility.* It is for that reason that I do not like the term *volunteer* when thinking of God's people serving the body of Christ. The term volunteer may give a believer the idea that he has an option whether or not he is willing to serve in a certain capacity and that if he chooses to serve in that capacity, he is going beyond his actual responsibility (he is "volunteering")—and therefore has done something meritorious.

Instead, God's Word tells me clearly that if I have been gifted in a certain area I have no alternative but to use that gift, serving with the strength God gives me, for the good of others. Such service should be performed joyfully, thanking God for giving me the opportunity to serve His body.

Our responsibility is to learn what our gifts are and to use them to the fullest. Our gifts do not have to be perfected in order to serve. That is a mistake made or excuse used by many, which keeps them from serving. Opportunity and need will help determine when our gifts should be exercised. Our abilities to serve in a certain area will surely increase with experience as we exercise our gifts. If we wait until we think were are fully qualified, we may never use that with which God has gifted us.

There are, obviously, believers who are trying to serve in areas in which they are not gifted, or not sufficiently trained or qualified. This is where we need the honest counsel of the church leadership and membership. If I do not have the gift of teaching, I would be wrong to insist that I serve in that capacity. If my voice and mannerisms are unsuitable for the church receptionist, I should instead look for other areas in which help is needed. Thankfully, God has not gifted us all in the same way. Yet, he has placed on all of us the responsibility to serve in the areas for which we are most capable, not as volunteers, but as His children, joyfully accepting the responsibility to serve our brothers and sisters in Christ.

Application

For Individuals:

1. Are you presently serving in some capacity in the church? Have you considered that as volunteer service, or as a privilege and responsibility before God?

2. Have you looked on the church with a "consumer mentality," thinking, "what's in it for me," rather than, "in what ways can I give my life in service to others?"

3. Are there other areas of need that you could and should fill?

4. Are you confident that you know where your strengths and talents lie? If not, have you consulted your fellow members and church leaders to help you answer that question?

For Groups:

1. Discuss areas within your church fellowship in which needs are going unmet.

2. How have the concepts of "professionals" within the church and "volunteerism" in the church been misunderstood by laymen?

3. Does a pastor have any differences in his responsibility to the flock from those shared by a layman? If so, in what manner and to what degree?

Meditation

Prayerfully think about the meaning and implications of Galatians 6:1–10.

MINISTRY!
I THOUGHT THAT WAS
THE PASTOR'S DUTY

"But encourage one another daily, as long as it is called Today, so that none of you may be hardened by sin's deceitfulness" (Hebrews 3:13); "And let us consider how we may spur one another on toward love and good deeds" (Hebrews 10:24).

One of the most common misunderstandings among church members is that we hire pastors as the professional Christians who will do all of the work among the members and then preach to us on Sundays. Yet, in the Word of God, the pastors are to equip the saints (believing members) for "their works of *ministry*" (Ephesians 4:11-12).

The two verses above from Hebrews are spoken to Christians—not just pastors. In the Hebrews 3 passage we are told that we are to encourage other believers on a daily basis so their hearts will not be hardened. Note that this encouragement is to be on a daily basis (not just on Sundays).

The Hebrews 10 passage instructs us that we are to consider how we may help others on toward love and good deeds. In order for us to do this, we must know the flock. Again, these words are addressed to believers, not just to pastors.

There are many other verses which instruct us as believers (and members of a local church) to be about the business of ministry among our fellow believers. We are told that pure religion is to look after orphans and widows (James 1:17), we are instructed to build up others (1 Thessalonians 5:11); to comfort others (1 Thessalonians 4:18); to encourage others (1 Thessalonians 5:11); to counsel others (Romans 15:14); to abound in love for others (1 Thessalonians 3:12); to bear others' burdens (Galatians 6:2); to teach and admonish each other (Colossians 3:16); to speak to each other in psalms, hymns and spiritual songs (Ephesians 5:1); to submit to one another (Ephesians 5:21) and to pray for each other (James 5:16).

These instructions, addressed to all believers, cannot be carried out on Sunday alone. They must be attended to daily as we serve among the members of our local body. When one uses the term "ministry" we ordinarily think of the work of the pastor. Certainly he has a special obligation to the flock, but the New Testament also calls on each of us to care for our fellow members, looking upon their needs as our responsibilities.

This caring could be carried out in their homes, on the job, at school, in the hospital, at a nursing home, perhaps even in a jail. It involves getting to know our fellow members and their families, learning what spiritual, physical and financial needs they have.

Often we have a tendency to spend time with those members who are popular and with whom we feel most comfortable, but usually they are the ones with the fewest needs. The most lonely and those who are all alone, are the ones who really need us. Perhaps that is why our Lord labeled pure religion as when one cares for orphans and widows, for usually there are no returns or reciprocity.

Here are some practical suggestions and considerations to help us to obey the Lord in the area of visitation:

- Don't expect the pastor to do it; look upon it as your responsibility.

- Consider it a privilege to serve the Lord and His people in this manner.

- Ask God to help you determine just how you can serve in this capacity.

- Set some reasonable goals or expectations; otherwise you may continually put it off.

- Choose a companion to go with you and to encourage your responsibility in this area.

- Make a list of those people in your congregation whom you do not know and plan to get to know them.

- Make a list of those people in your congregation whom you suspect have spiritual, family, physical, or financial needs.

- Determine the needs with which you feel capable of helping.

- Plan to spend time with these individuals or families. Keep in mind it does not have to be a formal visit. It could be just shopping together, picnicking or enjoying a hobby together.

- Organize others to help you with larger needs.

- Keep your pastors, elders and deacons informed of the needs, especially if you are not capable of helping meet those needs. Ask for their help.

- Certain personal needs will require confidentiality. Don't violate their trust by talking to others.

- Pray with these members. If exhortation is needed, do so firmly, but lovingly.

- Do not promise them help and then drop the matter. People who have previously suffered disappointment need to have those on whom they can depend.

- Do not promise the impossible. There will be serious problems—such as deep financial troubles, which neither you nor the church has sufficient resources to resolve.

- Always exhibit genuine joy and hope. Through Christ there should always be hope and joy.

As you work among the membership of your local church, you are going to come across a large variety of problems and needs in the body. They will range across the entire spectrum and will vary from individual to individual and from family to family. Here are some of the ones you will meet:

- Depression

- Anger

- Loneliness

- Marital disputes, separations, divorces

- Rebellious children

- Drug, alcohol and sexual abuse

- Immorality

- Financial irresponsibility, debts, credit card abuse

- Spiritual laziness

- Physical illnesses

- Houses and family schedules in disarray

- Unforgiving spirit

- Unemployment and despair

- Disinterest in church attendance

- Illegal activities, tax abuse

- Incorrect theology

- Lack of family prayer and worship

- Weak faith

- Lack of joy

- Grief over the loss of a loved one

- Wrong priorities

Obviously there will be many good things you will discover also, but this list highlights just a few of the various needs you will encounter.

Adam's sin had a tremendous impact upon the human race. He plunged us into sin, ruin and misery, and we are called upon by our Lord to help our fellow members as they struggle in this fallen world. But keep in mind the deep satisfaction you will find when you help others recover, and then get to see them keep the cycle going as they, in turn, help others.

You will not learn of these problems and needs on Sunday mornings. But you will become aware of their existence as you regularly visit among members and really get to know the people of your local church.

Application

For Individuals:

1. What percent of the membership of your church do you really know?

2. How can you best use your spiritual gifts among the membership?

3. Begin today making a plan to implement your responsibilities in this area.

4. List some names of other members whom you could enlist to help you meet some of the needs among the congregation.

For Groups:

1. Are you aware of any portion of the congregation that is being overlooked with regard to spiritual oversight?

2. Discuss some of the prominent spiritual and emotional needs with which your pastors and elders must deal.

3. In what ways can the members minister to the flock in order to take some of the load off the pastors and elders?

Meditation

Prayerfully think about the meaning and implications of Philippians 2:12–13.

COUNSELING ONE ANOTHER

"I myself am convinced, my brothers, that you yourselves are full of goodness, complete in knowledge and competent to instruct one another" (Romans 15:14).

In this passage the NIV uses the word "instruct," while others translate it "admonish" or "counsel." In all of these translations, Paul gives the Roman Christians credit that they had (through the Holy Spirit) the knowledge and spiritual ability to look after each other. In other words, they were capable of counseling one another regarding their obligations to the Lord, to each other and to the world around them. The majority of those Roman Christians probably had little formal education and many of them were slaves. Yet, Paul teaches them that they are to instruct, admonish, or counsel each other on how to live the Christian life.

In our culture today we are being told that we are individuals who can live life the way *we* want to. We do not need others telling us how to live. We are capable of going it alone and doing it our own way. Further, we especially do not need "self-righteous people, church-going hypocrites, religious fanatics, or some book written centuries ago" to tell *us* how to live. We are quite capable of making our *own* life decisions without outside interference!

As the church is more and more influenced by the standards of society, rather than the objective Word of God, this individualism and opposition to authority has become rampant even among professing Christians. The thought of other Christians interfering in our lives, especially *admonishing* us, would raise serious objections among many in our churches today. Despite that, Paul's words are timeless and are as much in need today as they were in the first century—perhaps even more so as individual personal standards have supplanted our objective standard of authority—the Bible.

Peter writes that God, by "His divine power, has given us everything we need for life and godliness through our knowledge of him" ... and through God's "great and precious promises" ... we "may participate in the divine nature and escape the corruption in the world caused by evil desires" (1 Peter 1:3–4). Peter is telling us that through our relationship with the living Lord and by His inspired Word, we have what we need to live the Christian life. We do not depend upon the standards of the world, psychiatric formulas and behavior studies. Instead, we need to know what the Word of God says and then to responsibly obey that Word. That same Word (properly interpreted and applied) is the authority for us to use in counseling one another. We are not to press our own opinions and subjective morality on one another, but rather the clear teachings of God's Word.

Paul tells us that "All Scripture is God-breathed and is *useful for teaching, rebuking, correcting and training in righteousness*" (1 Timothy 3:15). Paul's statement is set in the context of the elders who use the Word of God in training church members in righteous living. But the same principles apply to the individual member. His privilege and duty is to take that "God-breathed" (inspired) Word and use it, first in his own life and then in the lives of fellow believers. His duty is to correctly apply the specific commands and implied principles. These must never be wrenched from their context. As proper principles of interpretation are employed, the Spirit uses the Word to change lives dramatically. That is how we are to *counsel* one another.

Paul, in Galatians 6, gives us directions as to who among us should be counseling others. It is those "who are spiritual" (vs. 1). In the previous chapter, in verses 19–26, it is clear that the spiritual are those who are not living in the "acts of the sinful nature," (sexual immorality, impurity, debauchery, jealousy, dissensions, etc.) but rather those who are living by the "fruit of the spirit" (those who are generally characterized by love, joy, peace, patience, etc.) These are the members who are called upon to restore a brother who has been trapped in some sin (vs. 1). Paul goes on to tell us that we are to be gentle toward one another, to watch ourselves also that we do not ourselves fall, to carry one another's burdens (vss. 1–2). There is a proper way to approach others who need change in their lives; it is one of gentleness, patience and humility.

However, one is not to be so patient that he allows sin to go unchecked in the body. There will be those times when we say "enough is enough," and we must courageously call for change. New Testament examples can be found in the cases of Ananias and Sapphira (an extreme example, Acts 5), a man involved in immorality with his father's wife (1 Corinthians 5), those who were taking the Lord's supper in an unworthy and unloving manner (1 Corinthians 11) and Euodia and Syntyche, who were feuding (Philippians 4:2).

Counseling one another involves not only dealing with sin, but also encouraging those who are suffering from depression, discouragement, loss, or grief. Paul demonstrates this aspect of counseling in 1 Thessalonians where he encourages those who have had family members and friends who have died. (See 4:13–5:11; see also 1 Corinthians 15 where he talks about the resurrection and the fact that death no longer has a sting for the believer.) Peter closes his letter with wonderful words of comfort to those who, as a result of their faith, have been scattered, with these wonderful words of comfort: "And the God of all grace, who called you to his eternal glory, after you have suffered a little while, will himself restore you and make you strong, firm and steadfast" (1 Peter 5:10).

Paul gives words of comfort about the suffering we must undergo as believers. He tells us that we should rejoice in our suffering, because "suffering produces perseverance; perseverance, character; and character, hope. And hope does not disappoint us, because God has poured out his love into our hearts by the Holy Spirit, whom he has given us" (Romans 5:3–5).

Our roles, therefore, as counselors to one another are not only to deal with sin, but also to offer comfort and cheer. Further, we are to train and instruct others in righteousness (see 1 Timothy 3:16 quoted above). Our counsel has both a corrective purpose and a training process. Admonition by itself can create serious relational problems. It is when we take the time to gently train others in the way of righteousness that we complete the God-ordained cycle.

Here are some practical suggestions as to how we should counsel one another (though this is not to be construed as a complete list):

- Make sure that our own lives are exemplary. Not perfect! No one is! But our overall lives should be such that the people whom we are counseling have respect for us. Christ is clear (Matthew 7) that we should first clean up our own lives before we correct someone else.

- Always pray before approaching another person and when possible, pray with that person. Remember that God is the one who changes people.

- If there is a sin involved, we need to know clearly what the Bible has to say about it. We must make certain that it is a sin, not something that we must learn to forbear.

- If a fellow member is discouraged we need to find out the basis of that discouragement and talk with that person about the provisions and promises which our Lord has given to us in His Word.

- Often we will deal with people who have lost hope. Those people must be helped to see that through the power of the Spirit of God their lives and their outlook can be changed.

- We must encourage those whom we counsel to be in the Scriptures frequently. Leave with them directions to those specific portions of the Word of God which address their situations.

- We need to encourage those whom we counsel to regularly spend time in fellowship with and in service to a caring, local church.

- Enlist the help of others who will also come alongside them and who will befriend, counsel and encourage them.

- When there are matters to which they need to attend, check up on them to make sure that they are doing their part. If they have sinned against someone, direct them to seek that person out and ask for forgiveness. If they are spiritually lazy, remind them of their obligations as believers. Get involved with them, showing not only by words, but also by example how one serves the Lord. If they are depressed or discouraged, spend time with them; do not allow them to sit alone at home enumerating their problems. Talk to them about their responsibilities, but also help them to see their unnoticed blessings.

- Always be truthful with them and urge them to be the same with you. Unless you know the real problems with which you are dealing, you are stumbling in the darkness as you try to help them.

- Encourage them to take steps toward progress—not perfection. Notice their progress and encourage them that they *are* making progress. It is sometimes difficult for people with problems to take giant strides. Remember and remind them, that many small steps ultimately measure up to real changes.

There is nothing as joyous as seeing those whom you have counseled becoming once again useful members of Christ's kingdom. In many cases you will have also created a close relationship with that person, and will rescue a Christian brother or sister—and may have gained a close friend for life.

Application

For Individuals:

1. Are there members within your congregation who are known to be living in serious sin who need to be approached about it, or others who need someone to come alongside them with words of encouragement? If so, prayerfully think about whether you, or someone else, is best equipped to take on that assignment. Though you must help your brother who is in sin, you must do so with great patience and care.

2. Are you aware of some good Christian books that you should be reading which deal with this whole issue of Christian counseling? If so, plan to go through several of them during this next year. If you are unaware of such books, ask your pastors to recommend some that are true to the biblical concept of counseling.

3. Take some time to go through the Scriptures to jot down verses which speak of our duty to look after each other spiritually. Commit at least three of these verses to memory.

For Groups:

1. The worlds of psychiatry and psychology offer much counsel. Give examples in which their counsel has been unbiblical. Give examples of biblical counsel by those professionals.

2. What are examples of subtle and destructive counsel that we must avoid?

3. Talk about ways in which Christians have inappropriately counseled others.

4. Discuss other portions of Scripture which encourage us to counsel one another.

Meditation

Prayerfully think about the meaning and implications of Matthew 18:15–18, Romans 15:14 and 1 Corinthians 6:1–5.

CHURCH DISCIPLINE
A BIBLICAL RESPONSIBILITY

" 'If your brother sins against you, go and show him his fault, just between the two of you. If he listens to you, you have won your brother over. But if he will not listen, take one or two others along, so that every matter may be established by the testimony of two or three witnesses. If he refuses to listen to them, tell it to the church; and if he refuses to listen even to the church, treat him as you would a pagan or a tax collector'" (Matthew 18:15–17).

One of the least obeyed practices of the New Testament is church discipline. Sometimes it is referred to as the excommunication process or expulsion of a member. Often it is a concept that is completely foreign to modern churches. Many think it is cruel and unloving. There also have been situations where church discipline has resulted in lawsuits against the church.

Yet, the New Testament requires it. Christ Himself clearly teaches it (see above). It is to be carried out in a patient, loving, hopeful manner. When the process becomes harsh or mean-spirited, it becomes unbiblical and very disruptive.

The term "excommunication" sounds a bit harsh, especially since the whole process is designed to recover the brother. Actually, it is a disciplinary process and for that reason I prefer the term "church discipline." The word *discipline* implies putting oneself under another as a disciple—to learn. And in church discipline, the brother is supposed to learn what it is like to be considered an outsider and to earnestly want to return to full fellowship.

In addition to the Matthew 18 passage quoted above, there are other New Testament passages which instruct the church regarding discipline (1 Corinthians 5:1–6:11; 2 Corinthians 2:5–11; 1 Thessalonians 3:6–15; 1 Timothy 5:17–21; Titus 1:10–11; 3:9–11).

What are the basic principles, methods and steps of church discipline? The most basic ingredient is a desire to restore the brother who has fallen into sin. If that has been forgotten or neglected, only deep hurt and disgrace can occur. We want to recover the sinning member to full fellowship with the body.

The steps are clearly outlined by Christ in the Matthew passage:

> If your brother clearly sins (and you can see no repentance) you are to go to him privately, as lovingly as possible, to encourage him to repent. You may need to patiently approach him several times.

> If he refuses to repent, step two requires you to take one or two witnesses on a succeeding visit to help you bring the brother to repentance (and quite possibly for them to serve as witnesses to verify that the biblical principles have been followed in a loving manner).

> With the witnesses present, should the brother refuse to correct the wrong, the next step is for you to bring the matter to the church (normally the church leadership rather than to the congregation at large). The church must address the matter, make the determination that it is a sin for which public repentance is required, determine that the Scriptures have been followed accurately and then call on the member to repent. Throughout the entire process, the goal is to secure the brother's restoration.

> If there is no repentance, step four involves the actual discipline process whereby the church refuses to have fellowship with the brother until he repents. The purpose here is to help the brother to so miss the fellowship of his church and the protection it provides that he comes to hate his sin and turns to Christ for forgiveness. When repentance occurs, the church must publicly, completely and immediately grant full forgiveness and restoration.

When following these steps, more than one visit may be required. In fact, it may require several patient attempts at each level to resolve the issues. There should be no rush to judgment. The goal is to see the brother repent.

When church discipline is being carried out properly there are several additional attendant responsibilities:

- Confidentiality. At every step the matter is to be kept confidential at that level. For example, in step two the only parties who are to know about the matter are the individuals bringing the charge and the witnesses. This is vital. Violating this principle can cause great damage.

- The sin being confronted must clearly be a sin, not some vague complaint or personal preference. There must be a clear violation of a biblical command or principle.

- One must always approach a brother who is in sin with true humility and love (Galatians 6:1–5). To approach one with a spirit of pride is both unbiblical and counter-productive.

- The church must be consistent and show no partiality in carrying out church discipline. Each member must be treated equally with complete fidelity to the Word of God.

- Earnest prayer should attend every step. God is the one who grants repentance and He must be approached regularly.

- Disclosing lurid details of sins is not helpful and is often very destructive to both the charged brother and the church body. Great care should be taken in the public disclosure of such matters.

- The entire church is to be involved in the final steps, the urging of repentance and if there is no repentance, the actual discipline process. It does no good for the church to finally withdraw fellowship from the person if many of the individual members continue to fellowship with him as if nothing had occurred.

- Forgiveness should be immediate when the brother repents. Full restoration should take place when the matter has been cleared up. If the discipline process has been public, the forgiveness and restoration must also be a public matter. The whole church can then express the wonderful joy of seeing the process work and a brother restored. (In a case where church leaders have fallen, restoration to an office may take some time for trust in them to be restored. In some situations, a leader may never be placed back into a position of leadership.)

- Church discipline is very seriously frowned upon and often criticized or made fun of, not only by the public but also by a number of evangelical churches. Yet, it is Christ's command to His church. Our allegiance should be to the Sovereign One over our church body—Christ. We must be zealous to carry out His commands rather than fearing criticism by those who are not aware of these biblical responsibilities or by those who simply ignore them.

- Finally, it should be clearly taught that the immediate purpose is to recover our sinning brother, but that is not the only intent. A church that practices church discipline demonstrates to the world its desire for holiness. It is also a deterrent to sin among the remaining members and it brings glory to the Head of the church—the Lord Jesus Christ.

Application

For Individuals:

1. Does your church practice biblical discipline? If not, do you know why it does not?

2. Are there current situations in your church where discipline is needed?

3. As a member, what do you plan to do about those situations?

4. What are some of the wrong ways in which church discipline can be carried out?

For Groups:

1. Discuss sins which you think require church discipline and sins which the church should forbear.

2. What happens in a church when discipline is not practiced?

3. If a discipline case must be brought before the entire church, how much detail should be given to the congregation?

4. How should a church protect itself legally in our litigious society when it must carry out church discipline?

5. What should be uppermost in the members' desires with regard to a person under church discipline?

Meditation

Prayerfully think about the meaning and implications of 1 Corinthians 5:1–6:11 and 2 Corinthians 2:5–11.

HERESY
I MUST REMAIN ON GUARD!

"I know that after I leave, savage wolves will come in among you and will not spare the flock. Even from your own number men will arise and distort the truth in order to draw away disciples after them. So be on your guard! Remember that for three years I never stopped warning each of you night and day with tears" (Acts 20:29–31).

One person has remarked that every church is only one generation away from heresy. That statement might be an understatement. In the passage above, Paul predicts that even in their own generation and from their own church in Ephesus, there will be men who will arise and who will distort the truth. It is altogether possible that when Paul mentions "even from your own number," that he is talking about the eldership, not just the church. If so, he is warning the Ephesian elders that from their existing leadership there will be men who will later fall into heresy.

No church is exempt from this possibility. All one has to do is to consider the landscape of churches and seminaries in our land and compare their theology today with that with which they were founded. Individual churches, many seminaries and entire denominations have left the evangelical faith. Many of them no longer uphold the full inspiration and authority of the Word of God. They no longer believe in the miracles of the Bible. With them the concept of a final judgment and everlasting hell is a relic of the past. The exclusivity of the gospel has been watered down so much that it is no gospel at all. For many of them all roads of sincerity and morality lead to heaven. And, thus, the basic message of the Bible has been totally shattered.

Who is responsible for this sad state of affairs? Certainly it is the responsibility of pastors and church leaders, denominational leaders and the Bible school and seminary administrations, boards and faculty. But the responsibility also rests upon the members of local churches. They are the ones who support their pastors, the denominations and the schools. Without their financial support, none of these could exist. And so the responsibility to ensure that biblical truth is proclaimed can, in some measure, be placed squarely upon the shoulders of the ordinary members of local churches.

That requires us as members to know biblical truth and to know when error has begun to creep in. Often heresy begins in very small ways—a statement here, a question there, a new insight expressed, doing away with the church's doctrinal standards, using new language and methods to reach people, shying away from the hard sayings of the Bible, attempting to make the gospel user-friendly. Many of these things seem rather innocuous at first but, when given time, they often blossom into a doctrinal aberration and later into a full-blown heresy.

Church members must follow the pattern of the Bereans who "examined the Scriptures every day to see if what Paul said was true" (Acts 17:11b). Imagine that! Here was the great apostle Paul, probably the most knowledgeable Christian who ever existed, yet these people were described as "of more noble character" than others (vs. 11a) because they tested Paul's theology by the Word of God. If Paul's theology needed testing, surely modern theology must be checked very carefully.

As a member of the body of Christ, we cannot escape this responsibility. We can't say that it is up to others to make sure that we are going in the right direction. It requires that we know the Word of God for ourselves, if we are to stand guard.

Further, it means that we exercise the right, responsibility and the courage to face any pastor, denominational leader or seminary personnel with the truth. Proper love, respect and concern should characterize our approach to these men, but, nevertheless, we must zealously guard the truth which was "once for all entrusted to the saints" (Jude 3b).

What we are talking about here and what Paul was discussing in Acts 20, are the basic, non-negotiable truths of the Bible, e. g., the inspiration and authority of the Word of God, the attributes of God, the person and work of Christ, the Trinity, salvation by grace through faith alone, the responsibility of holiness, the day of judgment and the imminent and bodily return of Jesus Christ. These truths cannot be compromised for a moment! They strike at the very heart of the Christian message.

A word of caution at this point: We must be careful that we do not charge as heretical anyone who departs from our views on secondary or less important truths, such as the particular form of church government, the mode of baptism, Sabbath questions, or particular views on eschatology. It is not that these are not important areas, but they are not on the same level as the previous list. Christian love, forbearance and patience require that we allow for such differences.

When a member sees the seeds of heresy being sown, he must first work with the church leadership. If they do not respond properly, then he has the right and responsibility to take the matter to the entire church body (or, if one adheres to a Presbyterian form of government, to a classis, synod or assembly)—but only in the matter of serious heresy, not secondary or less important areas. The entire congregation then must address the church leadership. This, like all matters of sin, should be dealt with in a loving but firm manner as prescribed by Matthew 18:15–18 and 1 Timothy 5:17–21.

Heresy usually does not get better. Most often it gets worse. It is much like a fork in the road. If one takes the wrong fork, the farther he goes, the farther away he is from where he should be. That is what happened years ago with our liberal churches, denominations and seminaries. Had the members stepped up to the plate and demanded a return to the truth, rather than letting their leaders continue to go into the wrong direction, we would have far less heresy to deal with today.

Application

For Individuals:

1. Are you sufficiently acquainted with the Word of God to be able to recognize heresy when it is presented to the church? If not, what should be your next step?

2. Have you noticed any areas in your own church, denomination or schools of higher learning that do not seem to fit with what you know the Scriptures teach?

3. If so, how do you plan to deal with those matters?

4. List some areas where you might disagree with your church, but areas over which you should create no problem (matters of secondary or less significance).

For Groups:

1. At what point does wrong teaching become heretical? Give some specific examples.

2. In what manner should a church member approach church leadership if the member believes that some teaching in the church is unbiblical?

3. Locate and discuss some passages in the New Testament in which the writers are discussing heretical views.

Meditation

Prayerfully think through the meaning and implications of 2 Timothy 4:1–5.

HOME BIBLE STUDIES
AND CELL GROUPS

" 'Say to the owner of the house he enters, "The Teacher asks:
Where is my guest room, where I may eat the Passover with
my disciples?" He will show you a large upper room, fur-
nished and ready'" (Mark 14:14-15). "… They broke bread in
their homes and ate together with glad and sincere hearts…"
(Acts 2:46). "After Paul and Silas came out of the prison,
they went to Lydia's house, where they met with the brothers
and encouraged them…" (Acts 16:40). "Gaius, whose hospitality I and the whole church here enjoy, sends you his greeting" (Romans 16:23). "Give my greetings to… Nympha and
the church in her house" (Colossians 4:15).

For a period of time as I was growing up in America about the
only corporate religious activity was held at the church building.
That seemed to work well when the churches were smaller, when
the members lived in close proximity to the building and when the
members were friends and felt close to one another. But today with
the proliferation of larger churches, especially the mega churches,
members can get "lost in the crowd." Where the travel distance and
time can eliminate many church activities, smaller home Bible studies, accountability groups, care groups or fellowship activities grow
in importance to the local church scene.

In the first century, there were no denominational distinctives.
There was only one church per city or community. Some of those
churches were quite large. As an example, the Jerusalem church had
thousands of members. While they did meet in the temple court,
they also regularly met in small groups in homes. In the passages
quoted above we find clear evidence of church meetings and other
activities taking place in homes throughout the Roman Empire. The
"house churches" were indispensable because initially there were
no church buildings, as we know them today. Without these home

meetings, many of these new converts to Christianity would have had no place in which to meet together regularly in order to pray for and to serve one another.

Today, however, church buildings abound. Our problem is almost a reversal of the first century problem. We have the buildings, but often their sizes and the numbers of members frequently prevent members from getting to know and serve one another. To help solve that problem many churches are breaking their membership down into small groups which regularly meet in homes. The warmth of a small group and the comfort of a home are much more inviting to people. These gatherings are also more effective when inviting the lost or new people. Many of these people will shy away from a church building and a large crowd, but when invited to a home they seem to feel more comfortable about attending.

As a result, many churches are now dividing their membership into smaller groups of perhaps ten to twenty members, so that those members can meet together regularly for the purpose of prayer, fellowship, Bible study, discussion, common causes and accountability. These are wonderful ways for the members to get to know each other and to care for one another's spiritual, physical and financial needs in a personal and semi-private manner. As their lost friends attend, they can witness first-hand the church at work ministering to each other.

There are, however, some practices that need to be properly observed and some pitfalls to avoid, in these smaller groups. Here are a few of them:

- Members must be discouraged from substituting their small group for regular church attendance when the entire body meets to corporately worship.

- When a group grows to the extent that its sheer size makes it impersonal, it should be divided into additional groups of proper sizes.

- A group should not be formed, or continued, unless there is strong leadership.

- Always seek to involve every member of the group, not allowing some members to hide in the shadows.

- Never allow the group to develop a critical attitude toward the church, its leadership, individuals, or other Christian organizations.

- Seek to have the group minister to the individual's whole needs—spiritual, physical, monetary.

- Do not let any person dominate the time and discussions.

- Draw bottom lines on important issues; don't leave every discussion open to all opinions (leaving the impression that truth cannot be arrived at).

- Keep the time properly divided between the stated purposes of the group—whether it be prayer, Bible study, discussion, sharing needs, or others.

- Refrain from embarrassing members with questions or projects which are difficult for them, especially visitors or lost people who visit the group.

- Share the responsibilities with the entire group (according to their abilities and resources) rather than with a few who must carry the load.

- When possible consider moving the group from home to home—to help take some of the load off the host. It will also help members get better acquainted with others as they meet members in their own comfortable home environments.

- Encourage the group members to help clean up and rearrange the host's home immediately after the gathering is over. This will encourage and help the host and will actually facilitate additional fellowship time as they work together.

- Don't fall into a predictable pattern in the way the meeting is held, where things are always done the exact same way. Eliminate boredom before it begins by varying the schedule and activity from time to time.

- In the sharing and prayer times, make certain that things are not made public which are confidential, or where members (or others) could be hurt by public exposure.

- Encourage expressions of appreciation for those who lead and host the group.

- Start the group on time and close on time.

- Seek to plan other outings for the group, such as picnics, sporting activities or joint gatherings with similar groups.

- Provide babysitting for those parents who could not otherwise attend.

- Consider some common causes for service outside the group, such as a jail ministry, a rescue mission, meals for the community's needy, clean-up, paint-up, fix-up campaigns, missionary needs, etc.

- Never continue a group beyond its usefulness. If it is no longer needed or effective, close the group in a positive manner.

- Never allow a church faction or a splinter group to get started in these gatherings.

- Keep your church leadership informed of any serious problems, opportunities or significant suggestions which come up in your group.

No doubt, there are many other suggestions that could be listed, but perhaps these will be of some benefit for those who wish to serve Christ in these small gatherings. Meeting with small groups can be times of wonderful fellowship where Christians become close friends often for a lifetime.

Application

For Individuals:

1. Does your church encourage small groups? If not, what types of them would you like to see started in your church?

2. What roles would you like to fill in any of these groups?

3. What are ways in which you have seen small groups develop spiritually profitable activities?

4. What are ways in which you have seen small groups stray from their purposes?

For Groups:

1. Discuss why small home groups are helpful to churches today.

2. Talk about things that you would like to see happening in small groups.

3. What are ways that small groups can be harmful? Discuss ways these harmful things can be avoided.

4. Talk about some of the best small groups in which you have participated and discuss what ingredients made those groups profitable.

Meditation

Prayerfully think through the meaning and implications of Acts 20:20, Romans 16:5 and 16:23.

MISSIONS, MISSIONARIES, MISSION TRIPS

"While they were worshipping the Lord and fasting, the Holy Spirit said, 'Set apart for me Barnabas and Saul for the work to which I have called them.' So after they had fasted and prayed, they placed their hands on them and sent them off" (Acts 13:2–3).

That event, in the church at Antioch, launched what was probably the greatest and most successful missions undertaking in the history of Christianity. Over the next two decades the apostle Paul (along with his companions, Barnabas, Silas, Timothy, Luke and many others) went throughout the Roman Empire spreading the gospel, establishing churches, training and encouraging leaders, while writing a large portion of the New Testament in the process.

When we think about missions, our minds are most often drawn to what has been called The Great Commission given in Matthew 28:18–20. After His resurrection and before He ascended into heaven, Christ instructs His disciples to go (lit., *when you go or after you go*) and make disciples, baptizing them and teaching them everything that He had commanded. Then He promises to be with them always. That is a call to missions, but it is also a call to all believers that as they go throughout their lives and throughout their calling, they are to be about the business of taking the gospel to others. It is not just a call to "professional missionaries."

Yet, one of the blessings, which Christians have in local churches, is the opportunity to collectively support missions and missionary activities. The New Testament churches supported Paul and his helpers on many occasions—financially, prayerfully, with hospitality and by many of the members and some of the church leaders actually joining Paul on his journeys. We have similar opportunities today through the various missions programs of our churches.

My wife and I have had wonderful and varied opportunities to be involved with the missions programs and missionaries of our church. From serving on the Missions Committee, hosting missionaries in our home over the years and having been on short term mission trips in the United States, Mexico, China, New Guinea and Myanmar (Burma), we have discovered a few *do's* and *do not's* with regard to missions and sending out missionaries:

- Learn as much as you can about the particular mission field you are looking into; mission agencies, books and the Internet are rich sources.

- Learn as much as you can about the missionary you are considering supporting. Ask about his salvation, his theological positions, his training and experience, his family, his needs, his short-term and long-term goals, his plans for accountability and reports to his agency or church and his plan to regularly communicate with his supporters. Find out if he was commissioned by a local church, what that church is like and how they will shepherd him as a missionary.

- Make sure that he plans to be involved in a church on the mission field and to help in establishing churches in his chosen area.

- Determine if he has developed sufficient support before leaving for the field.

- Inquire if he has insurance for his family and emergency plans, should he have to quickly return home.

- Ask if he is leaving any of his family at home and if so, how long he will be apart from his family—and if that is a good plan for the family.

- Find out if he has a clear grasp of the pitfalls and disappointments on the mission field.

- Seek to determine if there are any serious personal sins with which he is wrestling that need to be addressed before he heads out to a mission field.

- Ask if his spouse is in agreement with his mission calling and if she is aware of the deprivations and loneliness which often plague missionaries and their families.

- Learn whether or not he has faithfully served in his own church before he asked to be sent out.

- Try to determine if he is properly gifted in the way he hopes to serve. For example, if he wants to do translation work, is he a linguist; if he wants to teach and preach, does he have those gifts; if he wants to administrate on the field, can he successfully handle a myriad of details at home?

- Ask if his plans are to help staff the churches with national leaders rather than missionaries having to staff those churches.

- As a church and as an individual, regularly pray for each missionary.

- As a church and as an individual, regularly correspond with the missionary (and his family). It often gets very lonely on the mission field. Insist that he let you know of their needs.

- Insist that he have sufficient furloughs for R & R and opportunities to reacquaint himself with his family back home.

There may be many other areas you would need to explore. Sending out a missionary into the mission field is a distinct and awesome privilege. But there has also been much effort and huge amounts of money wasted when some of those missionaries have received insufficient oversight by the sending organizations or churches. Christ wants us to count the cost and to be wise in the way we spend His resources. For this reason, here are some *don'ts* we need to give attention to:

- Do not agree to support someone unless you have developed much of the above information about him and his family.

- Do not agree to support someone unless you are reasonably certain that the church has sufficient financial resources to continue providing for his and his family's needs once they are on the field.

- Do not drop a missionary's support while he is on the field. Give him plenty of notice when a change must take place.

- Do not keep supporting a missionary simply because you like him; make sure that God is doing something worthwhile through him.

- Do not expect glowing reports, unless they are true. Mission work is often slow and difficult. Let your missionary know you want the truth, not pumped up mission reports designed to impress his supporters.

Churches (and individual Christians) have serious obligations to their missionaries. Those obligations go beyond financial support. They also involve oversight and spiritual support.

One of the best ways to accomplish oversight is for the members of the church to take meaningful, short-term trips to the field to work with their missionaries and, in some cases, to fill in for the missionaries to give them a break so that they can return home on a furlough.

These trips can help teach us what a foreign mission field is really like and some of the difficulties our missionaries encounter as they serve in that field. There may be occasions when you will learn that the missionary is not suited for that particular task, or that he has needs which you, your home church, or agency can address. In either case, you will be in a better position to know if your support is being used wisely.

Application

For Individuals:

1. Could God be calling you to a particular mission field?

2. Think about the mission work you or your church is supporting and find out if there is a short-term mission opportunity for you.

3. Consider writing some of your missionaries to let them know that you are praying for them. Find out from your missions committee what ways you can be serving your existing missionaries.

4. Have you thought about volunteering for your church's mission committee?

For Groups:

1. Discuss your church's mission program. What are its positives and negatives?

2. What do you think is the best way for a church to support missions? A percentage of the offerings? A faith-promise commitment by individuals? A certain amount going to certain parts of the world? The leadership deciding on a year-to-year basis? Or, another system?

3. What commitments do you think a church should make to a missionary? What commitments should a missionary make to the church?

4. Discuss your thoughts on the best way for a church to recruit missionaries.

5. If you have significant suggestions in these areas, discuss ways to properly make them known to the church leadership.

Meditation

Prayerfully think through the meaning and implications of Acts 13:2–3 and Romans 15:23–24.

Section Four

The Leadership of the Body

CHOOSING A PASTOR

"It was he who gave some to be apostles, some to be prophets, some to be evangelists and some to be pastors and teachers, to prepare God's people for works of service, so that the body of Christ may be built up" (Ephesians 4:11-12). "Here is a trustworthy saying: If anyone sets his heart on being an overseer (pastor), he desires a noble task" (1 Timothy 3:1). "The elders (pastors) who direct the affairs of the church well are worthy of double honor, especially those whose work is preaching and teaching" (1 Timothy 5:17). "As apostles of Christ, we could have been a burden to you, but we were gentle among you, like a mother caring for her little children. We loved you so much that we were delighted to share with you not only the gospel of God but our lives as well, because you had become so dear to us. Surely you remember, brothers, our toil and hardship; we worked night and day in order not to be a burden to anyone while we preached the gospel of God to you. You are witnesses and so is God, of how holy, righteous and blameless we were among you who believed. For you know that we dealt with each of you as a father deals with his own children, encouraging, comforting and urging you to lead lives worthy of God, who calls you into his kingdom and glory" (1 Thessalonians 2:7–12). "To the elders among you, I appeal as a fellow elder.... Be shepherds of God's flock that is under your care, serving as overseers (pastors)—not because you must, but because you are willing" (1 Peter 5:1–2).

Determining that one has been called into the ministry is one of the most important decisions that a man can make. It involves a lifetime of service, filled with a mixture of every imaginable emotion—ranging from intense sadness to deep joy—as the pastor attempts to shepherd people from all walks of life, often with serious and constantly changing personal needs.

And next in importance to the man's personal decision, is the church's decision that the man (or men) in question is the man (or men) who should lead their local body. It is important because God has given the parameters of his work and the necessary qualifications required of the man of God. For a church to put its stamp of approval on men to lead, it is saying that the church is in agreement that these men have met all of the requirements which God has stipulated and that they are a good fit for their particular local body. Such a decision carries with it a great deal of responsibility and, thus, choosing a man should never be done in a cavalier fashion.

Unfortunately I have often seen instances in which men have been chosen solely on the basis of their oratorical ability. Yet the biblical emphasis is upon the man's personal character rather than his preaching skills (see 1 Timothy 3:1–7; Titus 1:5–9; 1 Thessalonians 2:7–12; 1 Peter 5:1–4). Many preachers have a "call sermon," which is a message that they have worked on tirelessly and can deliver with great polish. This particular sermon is preached to prospective churches in view of a call to the pastorate. When that is basically all that the church members know about the man, great risks are being taken. One sermon is not a sufficient basis for this momentous decision.

There are many areas which should be investigated before a church calls a man to her ministry. The pulpit committee (or pastoral search committee) must do its homework very carefully, but ultimately the decision to call a pastor rests with the church members. And in order to make an intelligent decision they will need to have answers to many questions. For example:

- Is this man morally qualified to fill the office of pastor? (See the 1 Timothy, Titus, 1 Thessalonians and 1 Peter passages cited above.)

- Does this man have the education, training, or experience to fill the job?

- What has been his past experience in churches?

- Is this man qualified for and will he be satisfied to fill the particular role being assigned to him by the church?

- Does this man know the Word of God?

- Is he committed to the inspiration, inerrancy and authority of God's Word?

- Is he a man of prayer?

- Does this man's theology track with the church's theology?

- Will his style of preaching be acceptable to the church?

- Are there any skeletons in his closet which could potentially harm him and the church?

- Is his personal life-style one that would set a good example in the community?

- Does he clearly love his wife and treat her with respect?

- Will his wife be a credit to the ministry?

- Are his children obedient and respectful?

- Will he work well with the other church leaders?

- Has he read and is he in agreement with the church's doctrinal statement, constitution, bylaws and the church's stated philosophy of ministry?

- Will he fit in well with the membership and will he actively shepherd their souls?

- What are his views on marriage, divorce and remarriage?

- Will he maintain a proper balance between the various duties of the ministry—preaching, teaching, counseling, administration, writing, etc?

- Will he lead in carrying out the church's discipline program?

- Is he leaving his current pastorate under any cloud?

- Are his personal finances in order?

- Does he appear to be a man of both courage and vision?

- Can this man and his family live within the salary and benefits being offered?

- Is this a man whom the church can respect and follow as an example?

- Does this man have a servant's heart?

- Does this man plan to spend a lifetime of ministry here, or will this church be used simply as a stepping stone to another ministry?

This is not intended to be an exhaustive list. Each church will have its own particular questions which need answering.

Obviously, to be able to answer many of these questions the church must spend time with this man and his family. For that reason, it is by far the best method to grow your own pastors right in your own church family. Increasing number of churches are developing their own pastoral training centers within the church itself. They are offering seminary level courses on location and are also providing the practical hands-on experience within the church. In doing so they can begin to really know the man and his family and are in a much better position to judge his qualifications for the office.

But it many cases that is not a possibility. And when a church must go outside itself to find a pastor, sufficient time must be spent with the man by the membership for them to be able to assess the man's qualifications and character mentioned above. Sufficient exploratory meetings and discussions should be set up so that the members are satisfied that they know the man, his background, his family, his theology, his skills, his ministry philosophy and other pertinent areas of his life. To do otherwise is to strike off in the darkness and risk serious harm to the man, his family and the church.

The church also has a responsibility to be perfectly open and honest with the candidate about the church body. Are there current problems? Is the membership unified? What is the current leadership like? Is the church growing or stagnant? Are there lingering problems from previous pastors? Is the church seriously in debt? Will the church be willing to follow a new man? Do the members want someone who will be honest with them in dealing with their lives? Complete up-front disclosure must be made so the candidate can make an intelligent decision as to whether or not he is interested or capable of filling the need.

It is impossible to cover all of the bases in advance and even when there is an extensive investigation, there will still be some mistakes. In some cases the wrong man may still be chosen. However, such mistakes should be minimized by the appropriate homework mentioned above.

Obviously, the most important ingredient for the church and the candidate is serious prayer, asking God to superintend the entire process, guiding both parties to the right decision.

Application

For Individuals:

1. Look at the verses mentioned above and assess your present pastors to see if they are biblically qualified. If any are not, how can you help them be qualified?

2. Do you really know your pastors? If not, make plans to get to know each one of them, along with their families.

3. Are you aware of the many heavy responsibilities which your pastors carry? Are there any of them which you can help carry?

4. Have you felt that you were called into a public ministry? If so, what are your plans to prepare yourself for such a role?

For Groups:

1. Discuss how your church chooses its pastors. Is this a good method?

2. If, in calling a pastor to your church, you learned that there was an unresolved moral issue with him at his last pastorate, what steps would you take?

3. What do you think is a reasonable salary package to offer a pastor? Assuming that there are several pastors in your church, in a variety of ministries, how would you vary that package?

4. Do you think the church members should vote on hiring staff pastors, or is that an issue that is best left up to the present leadership?

5. If a present pastor proves to be unqualified for any reason, whether it is a lack of abilities, or a sin problem, what should be the church's method of dealing with these situations?

Meditation

Prayerfully think through the meaning and implications of 1 Timothy 3:1–7 and 1 Peter 5:1–4.

APPROACHING CHURCH LEADERSHIP

"The elders who direct the affairs of the church well are worthy of double honor, ... Do not entertain an accusation against an elder unless it is brought by two or three witnesses. Those who sin are to be rebuked publicly, so that the others may take warning" (1 Timothy 5:17–20).

Churches are led in a variety of ways. Some are led by elders. Some have a democratic form of government. Others may have a mixture of the two, or some other form of leadership. Whatever the system, there will be those who are placed in authority and are looked upon as church leaders. In that position they will lead by making and announcing decisions which affect the church. Some of these decisions will be popular while others will meet with questions and, perhaps, even resistance among the membership.

Members have a personal responsibility to see that their church pleases the Lord (who is the ultimate Sovereign over all of the churches). That means that there will be times when members must approach their church leaders about matters in the church, perhaps decisions which the leaders have made. How, and in what spirit, should we do that? Here are some suggestions:

- Look at the matter biblically. Are the leaders doing what Christ says in His Word? If the answer is yes, support your leaders. If you think the answer is no, plan to address the issue with your leaders—listening to what they have to say. You may be right in your analysis of the facts you have at hand, but you may discover other pertinent information as you talk with them.

- Look at the church at large. Even though these matters may not be pleasing to you, are the leaders' decisions best for the entire body's needs? If so, you must put your personal preferences aside.

- Pray about the matter and for your leaders. Pray for their wisdom, courage and their love for the flock. Pray for your own attitude, patience and forbearance.

- Do not criticize your leaders to other members. You may be initiating a schism or unrest within the church.

- Study the matter carefully. Pray that God will give you wisdom and judgment in those areas.

- Never assume the worst about your leaders. Go into the situation with an open mind, carefully listening to their positions.

- Ask for a private appointment and keep the matter private as long as possible.

- If you are convinced that your leaders are following biblical guidelines, support their position by your prayers, talents and tongue.

- If you conclude that your leaders are wrong, try to convince them with the Scriptures and solid reasoning (never with emotional intimidation).

- If you cannot convince the leadership toward a biblical change in direction, then determine if this is a significant enough issue to involve others. Does it involve essential biblical truth? Will it require you to go against your Christian conscience? If not, the matter may involve a minor area and your responsibility should be to live harmoniously with your leadership's decision. For example, if it involves their calling a pastor who does not believe in the historicity of the first eleven chapters of Genesis, then you must oppose that decision in as respectful a manner as possible, taking the issue all the way to the entire church, if necessary. But if it involves a decision such as going to two services in place of one, or changing the church-wide prayer time from Wednesday nights to Sunday evenings, you would be wrong to make this matter a major issue and thereby upset the tranquility of the church over it.

- Lead others to pray for and respect your church leadership (Hebrews 13:7, 8, 17, 18).

- If a woman is married, she should either ask her husband to approach the leadership, or perhaps the two of them go together.

- Finally, thank God that He has established leadership so that your church does not experience anarchy when there are important decisions that must be made.

There will always be some separation between the members and their leadership. That is inherent in the relationship between those in authority and those who must willingly submit. But there are proper ways to help bridge the gap and perhaps the above suggestions will help enable you to do so.

Application

For Individuals:

1. Is there a matter about which you currently need to approach your leadership?

2. If so, have you made this a serious matter of prayer?

3. Make a clear distinction between those matters that are critical and those areas which are simply matters of preference.

4. List several words to describe the manner in which you plan to approach your leadership. For examples: "respectfully," "lovingly," "optimistically."

For Groups:

1. Discuss examples of church leaders who are approachable.

2. Talk about matters concerning which you should approach leadership and matters which you should accept as they are.

3. Discuss examples of unapproachable leadership which might cause difficulties in a church.

4. Before you approach a church leader about a problem, what are the preliminary steps you should take?

Meditation

Prayerfully think through the meaning and implications of
1 Corinthians 13:4–7.

WAYS TO DISCOURAGE YOUR PASTOR

"Obey your leaders and submit to their authority. They keep watch over you as men who must give an account. Obey them so that their work will be a joy, not a burden, for that would be of no advantage to you" (Hebrews 13:17).

More and more good men are leaving the ministry. Their reasons may include a lack of commitment, a serious sin in their lives, a feeling of inadequacy, the pressure of public responsibilities, erratic and long hours or some other issue. But often the main reason is discouragement caused by church members; something which Hebrews 13:17 says should not occur. How do we discourage our pastors? Here are some ways:

- Listen to the Scriptures being taught, but don't obey the teaching.

- Show irritation when an important point in the pastor's message lengthens the pastor's sermon five or ten minutes beyond its usual length.

- Start a gossip chain.

- Always expect other members to do the work that needs to be done.

- Consistently show up to the church services five to ten minutes late.

- Tell your pastor that the nursery is not your responsibility.

- Be mildly negative about most leadership decisions.

- Go to the lake on summer Sundays rather than to church.

- Pay your pastor so little that he cannot adequately support his family.

- Start a church project but let it die by your lack of perseverance.

- Regularly fall asleep during the sermon because your Saturday nights are taken by late activities.

- Look on your pastor as a "hired-hand" rather than as the shepherd over your soul.

- Let your pastor alone do all of the home and hospital visitation.

- Start a squabble within the membership.

- Fear men rather than God.

- Talk frequently about the weaknesses of the church.

- Never let your pastor know that you are praying for him and his family.

- Complain to your pastor about others.

- When the leadership mentions important financial needs, keep your billfold tightly closed.

- Refuse to sing any of the new melodies.

- Always want to go back to "what it used to be like" in the church.

- Resent new people who come into the fellowship.

- Automatically assume your pastor's motives are questionable.

- Fail to realize that your pastor must keep some things in confidence and thus cannot explain some things fully.

- Assume that there is only one way to do things—and your way is the correct one.

- Disapprove verbally of the new pastor because he does things a little differently from the way you have been used to.

There are many others, but surely correcting these would be enough to keep us busy for a while.

Application

For Individuals:

1. In what ways have you been a discouragement to your church leadership?

2. Think about the ways in which you can encourage your pastors. Make a list and plan to implement them.

3. Think about forming a small prayer group who will regularly pray for your church leadership. But be careful that the meetings do not turn into complaint sessions.

For Groups:

1. Think about your pastors. Do you know if they have been discouraged? If so, what has caused that discouragement?

2. Discuss ways that you can encourage your pastors.

3. Plan a course of action for your group in which you will frequently demonstrate your appreciation and support for your church leadership.

Meditation

Prayerfully think through the meaning and implications of Ephesians 4:11–12 and Hebrews 13:17.

HOW TO LISTEN TO A SERMON[1]

"... but I gave them this command: Obey me and I will be your God and you will be my people. Walk in all the ways I command you, that it may go well with you. But they did not listen or pay attention; instead, they followed the stubborn inclinations of their evil hearts. They went backward and not forward" (Jeremiah 7:23–24).

Often pastors spend countless hours in the preparation of their messages in an attempt to make them as biblically sound, compelling and as practical as they possibly can. Yet, just like the Israelites of old, many members do not listen, or fail to listen properly. And like the Israelites, they go away following the stubborn inclinations of their hearts, continuing to go backward rather than forward.

There are ample warnings in the Bible about how we should listen: "He who answers before *listening*—that is his folly and his shame" (Proverbs 18:13); "Therefore, consider carefully how you *listen*" (Luke 8:18); "I have told you already and you did not *listen*. Why do you want to *hear* it again? ..." (John 9:27); "My dear brothers, take note of this: Everyone should be quick to *listen*, slow to speak and slow to become angry" (James 1:19). While these verses tell us to listen carefully to anyone who is speaking, they are certainly very applicable when listening to a sermon.

Listening is a thinking process. One has effectively listened when he has received and understood the message as the sender intended for it to be understood. Several "listening experts" list four steps in the listening process: *Hearing* (sensing the message with the ear); *Interpretation* (understanding the intent of the message); *Evaluation* (making a judgment of the message); *Response* (At times the Bible uses listening and obeying—or responding—synonymously. One

[1] Most of this material has been taken from a lesson presented to an adult class at The Bible Church of Little Rock (Arkansas) by Kenny Sutton. It has been altered and rearranged and is used by permission.

has not listened if he has not obeyed, see Jeremiah 7:23–24 above).
A good listener:

- Blocks out possible distractions and is not easily distracted

- Concentrates (listening is work) and avoids mind drift

- Anticipates but does not assume (does not jump to conclusions)

- Does not judge until comprehension is complete

- Recognizes his own predispositions, prejudices or biases toward the subject or speaker and attempts to re-evaluate his position (he listens objectively)

- Does not dwell on unfamiliar vocabulary, but rather continues to work at listening and attempts to comprehend the main intent of the message

Here are six very important ingredients in listening to sermons:

1. GET READY TO LISTEN

    - Get sufficient rest before the message so that your mind is not so worn out that it cannot listen.

    - Pray continually, asking God to help you to understand and respond properly to His Word.

    - Make sure that you have everything needed (Bible, writing pad, pen, etc.). Sit where you can see and hear. Make sure personal needs are taken care of.

    - Motivate yourself. The responsibility for developing interest and understanding is primarily yours before God. Make a conscious effort to be optimistic and interested from the beginning. Give the speaker your attention. If you don't have a good, immediate reason for listening to a speaker, you probably won't listen properly.

    - Be sure to read any assigned readings. A listener who has done his homework has better comprehension.

2. FROM THE BEGINNING, DETERMINE THE STRUCTURED FORMAT

(When a listener knows the structure of the lesson, comprehension increases.)

- Try to figure out how the speaker has organized the lesson. Does the sermon begin with a brief summary of the main concepts, themes, or ideas? Does the speaker give an overview of his outline? Did you catch the main headings?

- Adjust your note taking to the speaker. Each speaker is unique and each should be listened to in an individual way.

- Speakers tend to select certain words, phrases, or expressions to make transitions in their outline, to introduce examples and illustrations and to qualify their statements.

Transitions	Examples & Illustrations	Qualifiers
Next	For instance	In my opinion
First, second…	As an illustration	In all probability
Finally	For example	

3. DO NOT LET THE STYLE OF THE SPEAKER STOP YOU FROM LISTENING

- Judge content, not delivery. Style is the person's characteristic manner of expressing his thoughts. You may not like a person's style (too dramatic, too flowery, too fast, too slow, too emotional, etc.), but a good listener focuses on the content and knows that delivery is of secondary importance (1 Corinthians 2:1–5; 2 Corinthians 10:10; 2 Corinthians 22:5–6).

- A young teacher is still developing his style. Be patient with him.

- A good listener skips over delivery errors and tolerates bad habits in a speaker.

(The person who speaks with charm and a polished style may really be saying nothing, although he says it quite well. A person who speaks with an air of authority may still be dead wrong. The unpolished speaker may really have something important to say.)

4.   BE AN ACTIVE LISTENER—WORK AT LISTENING

- Remember that listening is work. Concentrate.

- A good listener anticipates, mentally summarizes and weighs the evidence

- Our thoughts can be faster than the speaker's words. The average speaker talks from 125–200 words per minute. The average listener can process 400 words per minute. Poor listeners tend to daydream and then get lost in the sermon, much like the rabbit that took a nap during a race with the turtle. Try to harness your thoughts during a message.

- Be aware of your predispositions and try to listen objectively. If your position can withstand the arguments of a speaker— good. If not, maybe you need to study and reevaluate.

5.   EVALUATE (Make a judgment on what is said.)

- Has the speaker interpreted the passage correctly? Has he supported his position? Has he applied the truths of Scripture fairly and correctly?

- How does this relate to me? What are the implications? Where would this logically lead me?

6.   RESPOND

- Ask: "What am I going to do with the truths I have learned or of which I have been reminded?"

- Seek to grow into godly living, not just knowledge. Conform to God's Word (Colossians 1:10).

- Persevere. Keep trying. We are closer now than when we first believed!

- Let your life be characterized by prayer for help in applying the Word. One speaker may plant, another may water, but only God can give growth (1 Corinthians 3:6).

Application

For Individuals:

1. Evaluate your own listening characteristics.

2. Are there changes in your personal habits that you should make in order to help you become a better listener?

3. What types of messages have been the most effective in your life?

For Groups:

1. Discuss ways which you have found helpful in listening to a sermon.

2. Do you take notes during a message? If so, have those notes helped you listen? Do you refer to them later?

3. To what types of sermons do you find it easiest to listen?

4. Talk about ways by which you have kept your mind from wandering during a sermon.

5. Though this varies with speakers, approximately how long can you profitably listen to a sermon?

6. Discuss some messages that have had the most serious impact upon your life. What made those so significant?

Meditation

Prayerfully think through the meaning and implications of Psalm 119:97–112.

THAT SERMON WAS WEAK!
HOW SHOULD I REACT?

"In the presence of God and of Christ Jesus, who will judge the living and the dead, and in view of his appearing and his kingdom, I give you this charge: Preach the Word; be prepared in season and out of season; correct, rebuke and encourage—with great patience and careful instruction" (2 Timothy 4:1–2).

Preaching is hard work. There are few preachers who can have a winner of a sermon every time, week in and week out. Here are some reasons why preaching is difficult:

- Done properly, sermon preparation is intense and demanding.

- Other valid church activities often cut into the pastor's time and energy, absorbing them to the point that intensive study time is unavailable.

- Preaching requires the ability to take the languages and customs of thousands of years ago and make them relevant to present day audiences.

- Peoples' attention spans are often very short and their minds can turn off a monologue very easily.

- In a sermon the preacher is trying to reach a wide variety of people and personal needs in a single audience (adults, teenagers, children, the highly educated, those with little education, those with pressing emotional and sin problems, those who seem to have it all together, those who know Christ as their Savior and others who do not have the foggiest ideas about spiritual matters).

- The preacher has to come up with different and helpful illustrations and applications weekly.

- The preacher must by observation, prayer and through the work of the Spirit, seek to determine just what is needed at that point in the life of the church.

- The preacher must address specific needs without giving undue offense.

- The preacher must realize his first responsibility is to His Lord and he must give the audience God's Word even when there will be some who will not want to hear it.

Obviously, there are other matters that make preaching difficult. In fact, some men go into an itinerant preaching ministry so they will not have to go through the difficult weekly grind of facing the same audience each week, requiring something new and fresh every three to seven days. It is much easier to have a few good sermons that can be pulled out, dusted off and preached over and over to different audiences.

The faithful pastor, however, who labors for years in the same congregation has taken on an important and arduous task. Church members can help in making or breaking his ministry.

So, what should we do when a sermon is *weak?* Here are some practical steps:

- Pray! Always pray for the pastor, his life, his family, his ministry and his sermons. Pray also for your attitude, your patience, and your discernment.

- Is the *weak* sermon a rarity, or has it become the pattern? If it only occurs every now and then, just realize that no one can produce an excellent sermon on every occasion.

- If the sermons are often weak, then you need to ask God for wisdom in what your part should be in helping bring about a solution.

- Doing your very best not to create a general dissatisfaction or problem, try to observe others' reactions. Perhaps your analyses or expectations are wrong.

- If you are convinced that matters should be improved, analyze thoughtfully what would help the messages to become more productive. Is the pastor's interpretation of the passages incorrect? Are his outlines forced or unclear? Does he fail to use meaningful illustrations and applications? Is his language unclear? Does he not give you enough meat? Or is his sermon too heavy for the average church member? Does he not apply the text? Does he go on and on, not knowing how to stop a message? Are his general communication skills just too poor for him to be in a public speaking role? Are there helps or courses that he could take which could possibly improve his abilities?

- Once you have made your analysis, ask for a private meeting with him. With love and patience express your concerns to him and provide him with your specific analysis. Let him know that you want him to succeed and that you will patiently pray for him.

- Give him a sufficient time to absorb your suggestions and to make appropriate changes.

- If, after a reasonable time you see few or no attempts on his part to improve, then you should ask for a meeting with the church leadership to discuss your concerns. Urge them to address the issues if they agree that there is need for change. Then give them time to help bring about the needed change.

- If little or no improvement takes place then you should ask the leadership to consider placing someone else in the pulpit. Perhaps the preacher should be re-assigned to another ministry in the body, recognizing that his gifts are not suitable for the pulpit. Another alternative might be for the leadership to select someone else to share the preaching.

- Should the leadership not agree with your analysis, you may be forced to one of two conclusions: Either your concerns are not widespread or they are not vital and you need to learn to patiently live with the situation, or you may need to move your family to another congregation.

- Under no circumstances should you create a problem in the body by spreading dissatisfaction, unless there is definitely a doctrinal aberration in the key areas of the Scriptures, or unless the church is tolerating known sin with impunity.

- Remember that a skillful delivery of a message is not the important issue. The biblical content of the message is far more important.

Keep in mind that preaching to everyone's satisfaction is an impossibility. A preacher cannot satisfy everyone, all the time, on all issues. Make sure that the hill you choose to die upon is an essential one. If not, you may be forced to realize that God is teaching you important Christian virtues, such as patience or humility.

Application

For Individuals:

1. Have you mistakenly complained to others about the preaching in your church rather than following the biblical way of handling such matters?

2. Have you considered how difficult it is for your pastors to preach well, week after week and how many different church demands there are on them?

3. Do you regularly pray for your pastors and their messages? Do you compliment their good work both to them and to others?

4. In what specific ways can you help and encourage your pastors so that their messages will be more effective?

For Groups:

1. What are some of the differences between good sermons and bad sermons?

2. Do you feel at liberty to discuss with your pastor possible improvements in his sermons? If not, why not?

3. It is hard for a pastor who preaches week after week, year after year, in the same church to have a winning sermon each and every time. How much slack should a congregation give a pastor in this area? Are you consistently praying for his study time, spiritual and physical health, and your own heart as you listen to his messages?

Meditation

Prayerfully think through the meaning and implications of Acts 20:25–38.

REALISTIC EXPECTATIONS
OF YOUR PASTOR

"… We have already made the charge that Jews and Gentiles alike are all under sin. As it is written: 'There is no one
righteous, not even one; … All have turned aside…. There is
no one who does good, not even one" (Romans 3:9b–12); "
'This is how you should pray: …Forgive us our debts, … And
lead us not into temptation, but deliver us from the evil one'
" (Matthew 6:9-13).

In the first passage above Paul makes it extremely clear that all
men without exception are sinners. When our Lord taught the apostles to pray, about forty percent of the prayer that He gave them had
to do with asking God to forgive us our sins and to deliver us from
the evil one. We all have much forgiveness to ask of God. Our sins
are manifold. That does not mean that God, through the sanctifying
work of the Holy Spirit, is not doing a work of grace in our hearts
to make us holy. But that work will not be complete until we reach
heaven. In the meantime, we must wrestle with the sin nature which
we inherited from Adam. That applies to pastors as well as the rest
of us.

Pastors are sinners. They have weaknesses and faults just like
church members. This is not to say that they are not to live as an
example to the flock (1 Peter 5:3) and are not to have met certain
moral qualifications (1 Timothy 3:1–7; Titus 1:5–9). But we must
be realistic about their sinful nature. They will continually do battle
with the *old nature* which is still a part of their lives, and will do so
as long as they live. Total victory over sin will not be won in this life.
Sanctification will take place; victories will occur; bad habits and
sins will be overcome—but there will be many battles to fight until
the day of glory.

Churches sometimes idolize their pastors and forget that they
are sinners just like everyone else. And so unrealistic expectations
about their pastors are formed. When a pastor falls into a sin, mem-

bers are shocked and often their spiritual worlds are turned upside down. They do not understand how that can occur. These men are their spiritual leaders and they are not supposed to sin!

I don't want to be misunderstood at this point. I am not condoning or making light of pastoral sins, regardless of how insignificant they may be. But I do want to emphasize the "humanness" of pastors and why we should regularly pray for them. Satan is delighted when a spiritual leader falls. He knows how to attack him at his weakest points. Because of this it is vital that members regularly pray for their pastors. They must recognize that their pastors are not perfect and always need much prayer support.

There are other ways in which members can have unrealistic expectations of their pastors. Pastors have personal, family and emotional needs also. They need friendship, fellowship, rest, recreation and some time away from their work. Since they are on call 7 days a week, 24 hours a day, often their hours are long and erratic. There are times when family plans must be shelved because of sudden emergencies within the church body. Illnesses, operations, deaths, sudden marital problems, the loss of a job and other pressing needs regularly come up within the body and the pastor is often the first one who is contacted. This means that the pastor must suddenly cancel or rearrange his family's plans, or his personal time, or other pastoral duties to help shepherd the flock through some sudden crisis. These are not things that occur infrequently; they are part of the pastor's everyday life and can wear him down over a period of time.

Because the pastor is the one who is there to encourage the members in their times of stress, seldom do the members realize that the pastors, themselves, also have times of personal and family turmoil. Pastors don't usually get up on Sunday mornings and tell the congregation that they have had a hard week, or that their family had some difficult thing to go through, or that they are facing a gut-wrenching decision of some type. Members often see their pastors and his family as ones who "have it all together." But usually they are a normal family that faces many of the same problems which the average member family faces.

Being realistic about these matters will help the members recognize how they can pray for, help provide for and encourage their pastors. It can also help them realize that sometimes the pastors cannot be "all things to all people." When a hospital visit is missed, or a

sermon that week is not up to par, or when the pastor seems preoc-
cupied, or forgets an appointment he had with you, or exhibits some
momentary anger, just realize that he is a sinner, has weaknesses, has
family problems and needs, and that he is struggling just as you are
to balance all of these areas properly.

Remember that your pastor and his family constantly live in a
fishbowl for all the church to see—and sometimes the sight is not
going to be particularly attractive. They are humans also!

Application

For Individuals:

1. Have you had unrealistic expectations of your pastor?

2. Do you pray for him regularly?

3. How can you help provide the fellowship and encouragement
   he and his family need?

4. When criticism of your pastor occurs, what should be your
   responsibility?

For Groups:

1. Have you seen your pastor sin? If so, what attitude did you
   have and what steps, if any, did you take? What should your
   attitude and actions be?

2. Discuss what you should do if a pastor's family life is in disarray. Give hypothetical examples.

3. Discuss criticism of pastoral staff and what proper steps should
   be taken if one has criticism.

4. List things you should pray about with regard to your pastors
   and as a group, pray for them at this time.

Meditation

Prayerfully think through the meaning and implications of
1 Corinthians 3:5-9.

WHAT IF YOUR PASTOR FALLS?

"Be diligent in these matters; give yourself wholly to them, so that everyone may see your progress. Watch your life and doctrine closely. Persevere in them, because if you do, you will save both yourself and your hearers" (1 Timothy 4:15–16).

Pastors are human beings who, like every laymen, have been born into this world with a sinful nature. And so they are going to sin—just like the other church members. At times they are going to become angry, they are going to say and do foolish things, they are not going to be perfect husbands and fathers, their selfishness will demonstrate itself and they will not always practice moderation.

There will be times when pastors will fall into grievous sin. Unfortunately, in our culture we read more and more of well-known pastors who have become romantically and sexually involved with women within their congregation or a woman on their staff, or ministers who have stolen from the contributions. Just in the last few years I have read of three pastors who were either accused, or convicted, of murder.

We hear of pastors who have adopted heretical views or who have turned their backs on the Lord and reverted to a worldly lifestyle. Such instances can grieve a congregation and often will help destroy one.

What should we do if our pastor falls? Since pastors occupy a public office their sins often become open to the public. Sin is sin, but some sins have more devastating consequences than others. A pastor who on one occasion is inconsiderate of his wife creates far fewer problems than one who has had a sexual affair with his secretary. Both are displeasing to our Lord. Neither should occur, but certainly they create different amounts and degrees of problems.

First, we must determine if the sin is one that we should forbear, or if it is a sin which requires some form of action. An isolated case in which a pastor does not properly discipline his small child should be treated differently from one in which the pastor fails repeatedly to discipline his teenage child. If a pastor fails to adequately prepare for one message it must be treated differently than the case where one habitually comes to the pulpit unprepared. When there is an isolated sin of a minor nature, we must forbear, as we would for the average church member. Where these are habitual, or wanton, or scandalous sins, we must be prepared to address the issue. Here are some biblical guidelines to deal with sin in the life of a pastor or elder:

- In 1 Timothy 3, Titus 1 and 1 Peter 3, pastoral qualifications are given. If our pastor does not measure up to those qualifications, we must address the matter.

- If private, personal sins are involved, we must follow the various steps in Matthew 18:15–17. That always begins with a private one-on-one meeting (or meetings) hoping that the matter can be totally resolved at that point.

- If pastoral sins are alleged, our 1 Timothy 5 passage tells us that we are not to entertain any such accusation except upon the basis of two or three witnesses. This is to protect his reputation and the reputation of the church ministry. No member should be allowed to gossip.

- If such sins are then to be brought forth, they should be taken to the board of elders so that they can investigate the matter thoroughly. Patience should be exercised by the accusers allowing the leaders sufficient time to investigate the matter and render their decision.

- Sins which have brought public disrepute to the cause of Christ, such as a sexual affair, financial corruption or falling away from the basics of the gospel, should result in the pastor being removed from the office. In some instances the pastor may never be restored to the ministry. Such cases would be determined by the repentance of the pastor, the extent of involvement, the damage done and the wisdom of both the leadership and the members of the congregation.

- A pastor must always be given the opportunity to publicly express his repentance and sorrow and to make whatever restitution is appropriate. The congregation should be led to express forgiveness upon his genuine repentance. There must always be immediate forgiveness upon repentance, but restoration to the office, if it is possible, can only be earned by a new and prolonged pattern of obedience.

Because pastors carry a greater responsibility to lead an exemplary life before the congregation (see 1 Peter 5:3), pastors' lives are lived in a fishbowl. Their families will also undergo the same close scrutiny. That just comes with the territory.

But, God's men have been brought back into His service. King David, an adulterer, murderer and liar was forgiven, though he and his family had to suffer greatly for his sin. Peter was re-established in the ministry and John Mark was restored as a useful companion to Paul. Often the restoration process is long and hard and many of the consequences of sin must be lived with for the remainder of our lives, but we must always remember that our Lord is in the business of forgiving and restoring people—even pastors who fall.

Application

For Individuals:

1. What are some examples of sins by a pastor that you should forbear?

2. What are examples of pastoral sins which you should confront?

3. What are examples of those sins which would require public exposure?

4. Regardless of the nature of the sins, what are some words that should characterize your attitude when any of these sins are committed by your pastor?

For Groups:

1. Discuss unspecified examples of sin by pastors and how a church, rightly or wrongly reacted.

2. Is a pastor permanently barred from the ministry if he has fallen into moral sin? Support your position by Scripture.

3. If you became aware of a serious matter in your pastor's life and you were the only member in the congregation who had this information, what would you do about it? Discuss hypothetical examples.

Meditation

Prayerfully think through the meaning and implications of 1 Timothy 5:17-20.

DISMISSING YOUR PASTOR

"Do not entertain an accusation against an elder unless it is brought by two or three witnesses. Those who sin are to be rebuked publicly, so that the others may take warning" (1 Timothy 5:19–20).

When I was a young man still in college I was called to serve in a small denominational church as the unpaid associate pastor. The pastor had been there only a short time. The church consisted of a couple hundred members, most of whom never came. Their names were still on the church roll, they still lived in the community, but to my knowledge they no longer attended a church anywhere. That situation should have been dealt with long ago, but that was a typical scene in that denomination's churches. On Wednesday nights only a few of the members would show up for prayer meeting and Bible study.

Early one week I learned that the deacons had called for a special meeting on that Wednesday night. I was not informed what it was all about. When I arrived at church that night, the building was packed with people, most of whom were the members mentioned above who had long since quit coming. The deacons announced that they were going to take a vote on "vacating the pulpit" (firing the pastor!). Apparently the deacons had rounded up all of the people still on the church roll, had expressed some displeasure about the pastor and had "stacked the deck" against the pastor. When the vote was taken, the pastor was overwhelmingly terminated on the spot.

Because of the disappointing and unbiblical manner in which the matter was handled and since the pastor was a personal friend of mine, I resigned the church that night. To this day I have not been given a reason why the deacons took that action. I suspected that it had to do with his theology, but no reason was given at the meeting.

Many serious mistakes were made in that situation! Just to mention a few: There should have been elders who were in charge, rather than the deacons. The pastor should have been informed of the charges against him and given the opportunity to answer them. Those members who showed up only for this vote should have had their membership stripped years earlier for non-attendance and non-support of the church. At any such meeting the charges should have been laid out very clearly and the pastor should have been given an opportunity to speak to the charges. If the pastor was involved in sin he should have been publicly rebuked (see the 1 Timothy 5 passage cited above). He should then be dismissed, or restored, depending upon the sin and repentance involved. Probably the worst mistake was that the church was never even asked to pray about the situation. It was handled much like a brawl at a company stockholders' meeting.

All of the matters and steps should have been taken very carefully and the church should have been properly informed rather than the deacons planning everything in secrecy. I could list many other mistakes committed by this church, but the point I am trying to make is that the whole matter was handled in a thoroughly unbiblical manner. It was a spectacle to the members, to the community and soiled their witness for Christ.

The church continued to exist for several years afterward, but never really thrived. It has now gone out of existence.

Can a church dismiss her pastor? Yes, but there are proper steps. And since such an action affects many—the pastor and his family, the members and their families, visitors, the community and often other churches far and wide—such an action must be taken with great care. Here are some non-negotiables along with some practical suggestions:

- Any charge against a pastor (elder) must be substantiated by two or more witnesses.

- Church leadership (the elders) should take the lead in pursuing these matters.

- If it is a private, less serious, non-recurring sin, the matter must be kept private.

- If it is a public, serious sin, dealing with the matter must be open to the church.

- The pastor must be given the charges against him and then allowed time to either defend himself, or to repent.

- There must be no rush to judgment. There must be a presumption of innocence, rather than guilt.

- The church must be called to earnest prayer about the matter.

- Great care should be taken that no gossiping or malicious rumors be started.

- It is wise to keep a written record or audio recording of all proceedings.

- In some cases in which a pastor is dismissed, he should be given a time for healing and restoration, and possible resumption of his pastoral duties.

- Since the pastor will ordinarily have a family, when a dismissal occurs, the church should keep in mind the emotional, physical and financial needs of the pastor's family. Often this may take the form of continuing all or part of the salary allowing sufficient time for the man to obtain a job elsewhere, or to resume his duties in the church.

There are undoubtedly many other steps that should be taken, depending upon the particular church situation and the reason for the dismissal. Handling such matters will be determined partly based on the nature of the charge. For example: Is the pastor's preaching ineffective? Has he unnecessarily offended someone? Has he been involved in some scandalous sin such as immorality, embezzlement of church funds, or open heresy? Is he lazy on the job? Does he refuse to be reconciled with someone; Is he mistreating his wife or children? Has he become a glutton? Has he gotten involved in some hobby or interest and thus is neglecting his duties at church? Is he bickering with other church staff or church leadership? Have his children become wild and profligate?

Each one of these possible causes of his potential dismissal must be dealt with differently and over varying periods of time, but they must be dealt with biblically in all situations. Dismissal of a pastor is a very serious matter. But when necessary, a church has just as much responsibility in this area as it does in dealing with a wayward church member. In fact, the potential for damage is much greater due to the public nature of the office of pastor. Therefore, when dealing with such matters the greatest amount of care should be taken to ensure that things are done biblically, carefully, prayerfully and with trust that God will honor a church which operates by His rules.

Application

For Individuals:

1. Have you been involved in a church where a pastor was dismissed? Was it handled properly?

2. If you heard that your pastor was involved in immorality, what would you do about it? If a few members thought his preaching was ineffective, how would you handle that? If you observed your pastor speaking harsh words to his wife, what would you do?

3. Have you prayed lately for each of your pastoral staff? If so, for what are you specifically praying?

For Groups:

1. Discuss unspecified examples in which pastors have been dismissed. Analyze what about the dismissal was biblically correct and what was wrong.

2. If a pastor were caught in an immoral act, what responsibilities would the church have toward him, individually and toward his family?

3. If a pastor is dismissed by the leadership of the church, should there ever be a time when certain facts should be kept from the congregation?

4. If a pastor is dismissed and the man should apply for a pastoral role in another congregation, what is the last church's responsibility with regard to sharing information with the new church?

Meditation

Prayerfully think through the meaning and implications of 1 Timothy 3:14–15, 1 Timothy 5:21 and 1 Thessalonians 5:12–13.

DEACONS
HONORED SERVANTS

"So the Twelve gathered all the disciples together and said: 'It would not be right for us to neglect the ministry of the word of God in order to wait on tables. Brothers, choose seven men from among you who are known to be full of the Spirit and wisdom. We will turn this responsibility over to them and will give our attention to prayer and the ministry of the word'"(Acts 6:2-4); "Deacons, likewise, are to be men worthy of respect, sincere, not indulging in much wine and not pursuing dishonest gain. They must keep hold of the deep truths of the faith with a clear conscience. They must first be tested and then if there is nothing against them, let them serve as deacons... . A deacon must be the husband of but one wife and must manage his children and his household well. Those who have served well gain an excellent standing and great assurance in their faith in Christ Jesus" (1 Timothy 3:8–13).

Whether the seven men chosen in Acts 6 were actually deacons is the subject of much debate. Certainly they seemed to fill the role of that of deacons, though they were not given the title "deacon" in the passage. However, there can be no question but that those mentioned in the 1 Timothy 3 passage were to fill an official office in the church known as deacon. Between the time of Acts 6 and the time 1 Timothy was written, the office had been clearly established and recognized by the early church. Paul is further establishing that office by laying down the qualifications of a deacon.

In many churches today the deacons are the actual leaders of the body. However, that is clearly not the biblical pattern. Elders (presbyters, overseers, pastors, bishops—all different words for the same office) are to be the spiritual leaders of the body (see Acts 20:17; Philippians 1:1; 1 Timothy 3:1–7; 5:17–20; Titus 1:5–9; 1 Peter 5:1–4). The word "deacon" means "servant." Deacons are to be the officially recognized servants of the church. Clearly God intended for the *spiritual* functions to be headed by a group of leaders known as "elders" and the *physical* needs of the body to be under the direction of the "deacons."

In Philippians 1:1, mentioned above, Paul addresses the spiritual leaders of the Philippian church (the elders), those who took care of the physical needs (the deacons) and then the remaining church members (all in the same verse). By the time Paul was in his first Roman imprisonment (in the early 60's of the first century—when he wrote to the Philippians), the two offices of elder and deacon were clearly recognized.

In the 1 Timothy passage (quoted above), Paul lists the qualifications for the office of deacon. If one compares those qualifications with that of the qualifications of an elder, the major difference is that the elder must be "apt to teach." This does not mean that a deacon cannot teach, or would not have that qualification. But it does mean that unless a man has the gift of teaching (either privately or publicly), he would not qualify for the office of elder. On the other hand, a deacon is not required to have that gift, though it is obvious that many do and it is a great blessing to the church to have deacons who can competently handle and explain the Word of God.

The words *deacon* and *servant* are interchangeable in the New Testament. All of God's people are to be servants to each other, but the deacons are to be the officially recognized servants. Their assignments can be manifold (and all under the general oversight of the elders). Here are just a few of the tasks they can handle for the church:

- Collect, account for and distribute the offerings

- Maintain the physical properties of the church—buildings, grounds, vehicles, etc.

- Care for the widows, orphans and other needy members of the body

- Pay the church bills

- Supervise the benevolence program of the church

- Determine the salaries and benefit programs for the church staff

- Purchase and supervise the church's insurance policies

- Create and maintain church budgets

- Provide care for those members who have physical and financial needs

- Supervise building programs

- Usher and otherwise assist at the services

- Assist the elders in the distribution of the Lord's Supper

- Provide transportation for those members who are not mobile

Many other areas of service could be added to this list and in the increasingly complex culture in which the church finds itself today, no doubt a very long list of deacon duties could be added to those above. The ideal, of course, is for every member to be assisting the deacons in these duties. The most important function of the deacons is to take the responsibility for these physical and financial duties so that the elders can devote their time and energy to "prayer and the ministry of the Word."

It should be noted that when Paul talks about the qualifications of the deacons and their office, he makes several interesting and important statements. He says that they are to be "men worthy of respect," "they must keep hold of the deep truths of the faith with a clear conscience," "they must be first tested." He also says that those who serve well "gain an excellent standing and great assurance in their faith in Christ Jesus." Clearly, these men are not to be put in the office simply because they are popular or even because they are willing to serve. Their high moral qualities, their reputations and their good understanding of the Christian faith are absolutely essential. Though they are not to be looked upon as leaders of the church (as are the elders), they are, after being tested, to be recognized as spiritual men of high standing. They must be willing to serve in the trenches by overseeing the meeting of the physical needs of the body.

When doing so, Paul says that they will gain an excellent standing within the congregation.

We are to honor these men, we should regularly pray for them and thank God that He has gifted the church with such hard working, sacrificial and honorable men.

Application

For Individuals:

1. Does your church recognize both offices, that of elder and deacon?

2. In what specific ways can you assist the deacons in caring for the needs of the body?

3. Do you have men in the office of deacon who do not meet the qualifications required in the 1 Timothy passage? If so, how should you respond to those situations?

4. Have you aspired to serve as a deacon? If so, have you expressed that desire to the church leadership?

For Groups:

1. Discuss the Acts 6 and 1 Timothy 3 passages with regard to deacons. Do you think the men described in Acts 6 were deacons?

2. What are the different roles and qualifications of elders and deacons?

3. Are female deacons biblical? Was Phoebe (Romans 16:1) a deacon? Give reasons for your position.

4. Are your deacons meeting the needs of the body? If not, what can you do to help them?

5. Have you expressed appreciation to your deacons lately and do you pray for them? As a group, determine how you can thank them for their work. Stop and pray for them at this time.

Meditation

Prayerfully think through the meaning and implications of Romans 16:1 and 1 Timothy 5:9–16.

Section Five

Gifts and Ministries in the Body

ASSESSING YOUR SPIRITUAL GIFTS

"But to each one of us grace has been given as Christ apportioned it. This is why it says: 'When he ascended on high, he led captives in his train and gave gifts to men'" (Ephesians 4:7–8).

In Psalm 68:18, the Old Testament verse quoted above by Paul, we have the picture of a sovereign who has triumphed over an enemy and who is now returning to his country with a train of his captives. He is parading both the captives and the plundered goods which he has received before his own people. As he does so, he distributes these goods as gifts to his people.

Similarly, Jesus has triumphed over His enemy, the devil, and now He has ascended to the Father in heaven. In doing so, He has given out gifts to His people, the church, by distributing abilities, special interests and opportunities, which are to be trained, perfected and used for the good of the church collectively (see Romans 12:1–16; 1 Corinthians 12:1–30; Ephesians 4:7–16; 1 Peter 4:7–11).

Paul, in Ephesians 4, lists some of these gifts and discusses how they are to be developed and used. Specifically, the pastors/teachers (themselves gifts to the church) are to prepare the members to use their gifts ("to prepare God's people for their works of service," vs. 12).

In Romans 12: 4–8 the apostle Paul clearly states that all believers have received a gift (or gifts) and that we are under obligation to use them for building up the church. One person has remarked that there are to be no drones in the body of Christ. All of us are to have an active part as workers.

But what part? Many Christians do not seem to know what their spiritual gifts are. Others believe that they must discern the one particular gift with which they have been entrusted before they can adequately serve. Often they go through life dissatisfied and frustrated because they do not know what that gift is. How, then, can a child of God determine the particular service he has been called to?

Some would break the various gifts into specific categories. For example, there is a view that says all gifts can be broken down into only two general areas: speaking and serving (see 1 Peter 4:11). Other breakdowns would give us several major areas, such as prophecy (teaching, preaching), administration, mercy, admonition, serving and other areas.

Some would say that the Bible only gives us examples of gifts and not exhaustive lists. They argue that if the Word of God were to list all of the specific gifts that it would be outdated and incomplete quickly because in each culture and age the needed gifts change.

How, then, can we set down some basic biblical principles which do not change and which will help us assess our gifts? Here are some principles with which to begin:

- By grace, Christ apportions His gifts (Ephesians 4:7–13).

- Each believer has been given one or more gifts (Romans 12:1–8).

- These gifts belong to the body, not to the individual (Romans 12:5).

- We will be held responsible as to how faithful we are in the development and use of these gifts (Matthew 25:14–30; 2 Corinthians 5:10).

- Pastors/teachers are to be the ones who prepare God's people for their works of service (the use of their gifts) (Ephesians 4:11–13).

- Gifts, properly used, help build up the body of Christ (Ephesians 4:13).

- Gifts, properly used, help protect the body of Christ (Ephesians 4:14).

- Gifts, properly used, administer God's grace to His people (1 Peter 4:10).

- Properly using gifts will be rewarded at the Day of Judgment (Matthew 25:14–30; 2 Corinthians 5:10).

Seeing, then, that gifts are vitally important, how do we know what our gifts are? And can they change or develop over the years? The answers to these questions are not difficult and mysterious. A knowledge of the Word of God, an awareness of the needs around us and a bit of common sense should help us answer these questions.

First, what gifts have I received? Answer these questions: (1) What can I accomplish with my present abilities? (2) What type of service am I personally drawn to? (3) What have I been educated or trained to do? (4) What gifts do my pastors and church leaders think that I possess? (5) What does my family (who should know me best) think that my gifts are? (6) What specific needs are there in the church body? (7) Have I attempted to use a gift in a certain area and have regularly failed? (8) When have I met with success in attempting to exercise a gift or meet a need in the body? (9) Have I asked my closest friends to honestly help assess where I could most successfully serve—whether it be leadership, teaching, deacon work, benevolence activities, helping maintain the church building and grounds, counseling, nursery work, or other service areas?

One of the best methods of trying to determine where and in what manner we should serve is by seeking the counsel of godly people. Here are some of the verses in Proverbs which tell us of the wisdom of seeking counsel: Proverbs 1:25, 30–33; 12:15; 13:10; 15:22; 19:20–21; 20:18; 27:9.

Our second question is "will my gifts change or develop over the years?" Certainly they can develop. We only have to look at a few biblical examples. Timothy began as a student and traveling companion to Paul. He later became a pastor and a church leader (1 Timothy 1–5; 2 Timothy 2:1–4:8). Titus is another example of one who began on the fringes but later developed into a spiritual leader. He was charged by the apostle Paul to appoint elders in the churches of Crete and to maintain correct theology and right living (Titus 1:5–3:11). The apostle John was originally known as a "son of thunder" because of his explosive personality (Luke 9:54), yet he later became the elder statesman whose constant message was to love one another (1 John 3:11). Peter was an example of impetuosity (Matthew 26:31–35), but later became the stable elder who called on his fellow elders to live as examples before the flock (2 Peter 5:1–4). John Mark left the service at Paul's side (Acts 13:13), but later became useful to him (2 Timothy 4:11).

Gifts, therefore, can develop with spiritual growth, maturity, education, training and experiences.

Will gifts change? Is a person born with a natural gift—a certain propensity or personality which he carries to the grave? For example, are there natural born leaders who would always fail in the area of a mercy or helping ministries, who, when given the opportunity to lead, would always shine? Or, are there people who will always best fit in a private role giving mercy, who would never be able to effectively lead a group? Can we always fit a person into his gift role based on his personality type? And what about personality tests? Can a church depend upon them as the best indicator of where a person should serve within the congregation?

Perhaps more basic to all of these questions is: What is a gift? Is it something with which a person is born (and, therefore, would not change and could be predicted based on a personality or a gifts test)? Is it supernaturally bestowed by God upon His people? Or, is it something which a person must learn over a period of time? Or, does it come quite naturally to a person only after he has been given the opportunity to serve?

First, we need to address the issue of personality and gifts tests. In my opinion, trying to make gift assessments based on these factors alone can be risky. People can reflect different personalities in different situations. Some people may misunderstand the questions and mistakenly answer them. Others may force certain answers hoping for certain results. Answers can be misread and misapplied. Therefore, to rely solely on personality tests to help a person determine his life's service to God could be a serious mistake.

I also believe that personalities can change over a period of time, therefore, we should be very careful about confining people to a narrow range of service. God changes people. He is in the very business of changing people—their personalities, their methods and their desire to serve.

For example, an angry, over-bearing, high-powered executive can be born again by the Spirit of God and be given the desire to meekly and joyfully serve others in a private role where there is no public exposure. And he may find complete contentment in that capacity for the remainder of his days here on earth. One may say, "What a waste of talent or gift." Yet God may have given this man the gift of a humble spirit who wants to serve others.

There are people who, if placed in leadership, would at that time be in a totally inappropriate role. But who is to say that by God's grace, with education, training and tried exposure, that they could never be effective leaders? Some might say, "I don't have the gift of preaching, or could never see myself serving in any other leadership role and I don't think I could ever fit into one of those areas." Think again. Are you sure that given the time, education and training, that you could never be equipped for one of those areas? You might respond, "Well, I have never even had a desire for such a role." But what if you were genuinely needed by the body to serve in that capacity? Would you refuse to try to add to your abilities in these areas in order to help meet the needs of the body? Would not Christ want you to do everything you could, within Scriptural guidelines, to assist your congregation?

Trying to put many biblical concepts together, I would define a *gift* as a combination of personal desire, natural propensities and learned abilities. Obviously, all of this must be given to us by the grace of God, hence a *gift*. And for that reason they are often spoken of as "grace-gifts."

And so I would conclude that gifts can change, as our Lord changes us over the years and as He shows us the necessity to serve the body of Christ in whatever way needed.

As a concluding example, let's suppose the pastor of a church (we'll call him "Joe") is strongly gifted in preaching and has concluded that preaching is his main gift within the body. All of his efforts are being expended in that area and the church is being blessed by his concentrated effort. And then someone else is added to the congregation (we'll call him Sam) who is even more gifted in the area of preaching. It has been noted over the years that Joe has some abilities in administration and the church now has grown to the point that it needs an administrator. With some concentrated training, Joe could probably be equipped to fill that need very well. Would we not be led to the conclusion that perhaps Joe and Sam could co-pastor the church, with Joe spending some of his time as a gift to the body as a much needed and capable administrator?

Opportunities and church needs may actually help us discover what our gifts are. If our obligation within the body is to serve others, then we should always be open to the possibility of serving wherever we are needed, within biblical guidelines, with whatever abilities we have, or can be trained to have.

Application

For Individuals:

1. What spiritual gift(s) has the Lord given you?

2. In what specific ways are you using your spiritual gift(s) in your congregation?

3. What are you doing to further develop your gift(s)?

4. If you are unsure as to where and how you should serve, make a list of those leaders and/or members from whom you plan to seek advice.

For Groups:

1. Look at the four passages, Romans 12, 1 Corinthians 12, Ephesians 4 and 1 Peter 4 and discuss the various gifts mentioned in these passages.

2. Discuss whether these are the only gifts possible, or if they appear to be examples of gifts.

3. Discuss helpful ways in which gifts can be used in your congregation. Do you and the group encourage those whom you know as they use their gifts?

Meditation

Prayerfully think through the meaning and implications of 1 Corinthians 13.

THE MANY "ONE ANOTHERS" OF THE NEW TESTAMENT

"Besides everything else, I face daily the pressure of my concern for all the churches. Who is weak and I do not feel weak? Who is led into sin and I do not inwardly burn" (2 Corinthians 11:28–29).

The church is not a club or organization where one demonstrates one's talents or creative ability in order to receive the acclaim of the other members. Instead it is a body in which each member has mutual responsibilities toward both the other individuals and the whole. The Bible calls for this in the many *one anothers* throughout its pages. Here is a list of the major ones:

- Don't judge *one another* (Romans 14:13).

- Wait for *one another* at the Lord's table (1 Corinthians 11:33).

- Accept *one another* (Romans 15:7).

- Confess your sins to *one another* (James 5:16).

- Build up *one another* (1 Thessalonians 5:11).

- Be of the same mind as *one another* (Romans 12:16).

- Comfort *one another* (1 Thessalonians 4:18).

- Employ your spiritual gift in serving *one another* (1 Peter 4:10).

- Pray for *one another* (James 5:16).

- Be devoted to *one another* (Romans 12:10).

- Be at peace with *one another* (Mark 9:50).

- Encourage *one another* (1 Thessalonians 5:11).

- Accept *one another* (Romans 15:7).

- Greet *one another* with a holy kiss—Romans 15:16

- Don't become boastful in challenging *one another* (Galatians 5:26).

- Don't be envying *one another* (Ephesians 4:32).

- Be kind to *one another* (Ephesians 4:32).

- Abound in love for *one another* (1 Thessalonians 3:12).

- Live in peace with *one another* (1 Thessalonians 5:13).

- Fervently love *one another* from the heart (1 Peter 1:22).

- Have fellowship with *one another* (1 John 1:7).

- Don't hate *one another* (Titus 3:3).

- We are individually members of *one another* (Romans 12:5).

- Love *one another* (John 13:34).

- Regard *one another* as more important than yourself (Philippians 2:3).

- Bear *one another's* burdens (Galatians 6:2).

- Admonish *one another* (Romans 15:14).

- Serve *one another* (Galatians 5:13).

- Do not lie to *one another* (Colossians 3:9).

- Bear with *one another* (Colossians 3:13).

- Teach and admonish *one another* (Colossians 3:16).

- Don't repay *one another* with evil (1 Thessalonians 5:15).

- Care for *one another* (1 Corinthians 12:25).

- Be devoted to *one another* (Romans 12:10).

- Clothe yourselves with humility toward *one another* (1 Peter 5:5).

- Don't forsake assembling with *one another* (Hebrews 10:24).

- Do not speak against *one another* (James 4:11).

- Be hospitable to *one another* without complaint (1 Peter 4:9).

- Don't have lawsuits with *one another* (1 Corinthians 6:7).

- Speak to *one another* in psalms, hymns and spiritual songs (Ephesians 5:19).

- Do not complain against *one another* (James 5:9).

- Show forbearance to *one another* (Ephesians 4:2).

- Give preference to *one another* (Romans 12:10).

- Don't bite and devour *one another* (Galatians 5:15).

- Submit to *one another* in the fear of Christ (Ephesians 5:21).

- Seek the good of *one another* (1 Thessalonians 5:15).

- Stimulate *one another* to love and good deeds (Hebrews 10:23).

These are not theoretical ideas, but daily, practical responsibilities toward our fellow members. We live in a world where rugged individualism has become the norm. More and more we see less and less interaction among people. Often even our next door neighbors are strangers to us. Television occupies our time and we sit in front of it isolated from the rest of the world. In addition, home architecture has contributed to this isolation. Homes now usually have small front porches and instead, large decks or patios in the rear of the homes. Surrounded by walls or privacy fences, our world at home consists of television or back yard activities. And now the latest interruption of our interaction with people is the preoccupation with the Internet, where people spend hours and hours before a screen, cutting themselves off from personal relationships with others.

Gone are the days when we sat on our front porches visiting with the neighbors from across the street or down the street. When I was growing up in the forties and fifties, Sunday afternoons were spent making homemade ice cream for the neighborhood, with a yard softball game or some other activity going on at the same time. We knew the people next door, down the street, across the street and in our vicinity.

This similar pattern of isolation has emerged in our churches. Many members attend the services, put in their offerings and then go home to their cloistered environment. Little attention is given to the mutual responsibilities of the Bible—the one anothers.

Someone has said that real joy as a Christian comes from this little formula: J O Y: Jesus first, Others second and Yourself last. There can be no better way to have joy than to assess our gifts and determine which of the "one anothers" we can best obey. To an extent, all of them are our responsibility but we may have a special gift in certain of these areas. If we cannot determine for ourselves what our gift is, we should ask our pastors, our family or a close companion to help us make a proper assessment. Once that is determined, then we should be about the business of learning where true joy comes from—putting Christ and others above ourselves.

Application

For Individuals:

1. What happens in a congregation when these "one anothers" are ignored?

2. Make a list of some of the above "one anothers" which you want to put into practice in your church fellowship.

3. Think about asking your church leadership to develop a study or a series of messages dealing with some of the more needed "one anothers" in your church body.

For Groups:

1. Discuss ways in which the various members of your group can put these "one anothers" into practice within your group or church.

2. Which of these "one anothers" are the easiest and which are the most difficult to obey?

3. What happens to a church when its members are not aware that these "one anothers" are their responsibility?

4. If your church is not obeying these commands, how would you go about helping your church become aware of these responsibilities? Discuss these ways.

Meditation

Prayerfully think through the meaning and implications of Romans 12:1.

EVERY MEMBER IS A MINISTER

"It was he who gave some to be apostles, some to be prophets, some to be evangelists, and some to be pastors and teachers, to prepare God's people for works of service, so that the
body of Christ may be built up" (Ephesians 4:11–12).

In the passage quoted above, when it speaks of preparing God's
people for *works of service*, several translations render it "for their
ministry." The thought is the same. Members of local churches must
be involved in the ministry.

Too often we think of the staff (pastors and support personnel) as
the professional Christians at the church who are supposed to be the
ones who conduct God's business through the church. They are the
ones who should do the preaching, administer the ordinances, visit
the sick, make home visits, preach the funerals, perform weddings,
do the counseling and take care of the administration areas of the
church, along with a host of other duties. The members are looked
upon as those who attend, pay the expenses by their contributions,
vote on who will serve as pastors and then decide when there should
be a change in the leadership.

Yet, that is not God's view of how His church should be run. In
the verse quoted above, the members are the ones who actually do
the ministry. The pastors/teachers are God's gift to the church to
equip the members (the ministers) to do their *works of service.*

God never intended for the pastors to do all of the teaching,
the physical handling of the church property, all of the counseling,
all of the hospital and home visitation, all of the planning, all of the
evangelizing, all of the visiting of the widows and orphans and all
the day-to-day ministries of the church.

Somehow in our culture this state of affairs has crept into many
of our churches. Part of the blame can be laid at the feet of pastors who have not sufficiently taught the members that they also are
ministers. On many occasions *laymen* are better gifted or equipped
to do certain aspects of the ministry than those who are considered
the professionals. Laymen are often better personal evangelists simply

because they can approach others on the same level. People automatically erect a wall between themselves and a pastor. Often people feel very awkward, shy, or defensive when a pastor begins to speak with them. A layman does not have to try to get through that barrier. This common misconception is summarized in the humorous remarks sometimes made to laymen: "We pastors get paid for being good; you're good for nothing." People generally respect a lay person who is faithful and dedicated to his calling, whereas pastors lack such admiration and respect because people think they are simply doing "what they get paid to do."

Evangelism is an important, but by no means the only important area in which laymen must be involved. In fact, their areas of ministry cover such a broad field that we can only scratch the surface here. The following list is not complete, but suggestive. If you have not yet found your *ministry*, think about some of these possibilities. God wants you to fully support your pastors and other church leaders, but He also instructs you to find, develop and use your own ministry skills.

Here are some ministry areas to consider:

- Pastor/Elder (Perhaps God is calling and equipping you to be a spiritual leader of the body.)

- Deacon (Has God equipped you to help take care of the building, grounds, finances or to serve orphans and widows, or other needy people?)

- Participate in an evangelism program.

- Teach or assist in Sunday School, either adults or children.

- Work in the nursery.

- Do maintenance work on the building or grounds.

- Help operate the tape program.

- Learn to operate the church sound system.

- Be involved in the music ministry (adult choir, orchestra, children's choir).

- Work on the Women's Ministry Committee.

- Offer to work in the church office.

- Work with the leader of a Home Cell Group or offer your home for meetings.

- Work with the youth program.

- Lead a regular prayer group.

- Lead a small Bible study.

- Serve as a Sunday greeter.

- Visit members and visitors in their homes.

- Visit those in the hospitals, the elderly, the shut-ins.

- Serve on a church construction crew.

- Plan, lead or serve in a short-term mission trip.

- Help raise money for special events and programs.

- Offer to help the church treasurer.

- Offer to help keep up the membership roster.

- Serve as the librarian, or help in the library.

- Offer your home for missionaries, visiting speakers or the homeless.

- Offer to do yard work for the elderly members of the church.

- Offer your particular skills to members, such as carpentry, plumbing, electrical work or auto repairs.

- Prepare and serve food for special church activities.

- Take youth, children and the elderly on special outings.

- Serve in the church benevolence program.

- Serve in the inner-city ministry of the church.

- Work in the church's food bank or food distribution program.

- Lead or serve on a jail, prison evangelistic team or Bible teaching team.

- Be the church photographer.

- Write letters and send material to foreign missionaries to keep them up-to-date.

- Serve on a church committee (Building, Nominating, Pulpit, Finance, or Missions Committees).

- If you are qualified in certain areas, offer to provide counsel to those with problems or needs.

No doubt many important areas of ministry have been left out. There is so much ministry to be conducted by God's churches that it is clear that the "professionals" cannot do it alone. Their God-given responsibility is to prepare the members for *their ministries*. In that sense, every member is a *minister*!

Application

For Individuals:

1. Are you satisfied that you are serving in a needed ministry in your church? If not, look over the list in this article and see if you could select one for which you are suited, then contact your church leadership and offer your service.

2. Are there ways in which you can help some of your fellow members to see that they, also, are ministers who should be involved in a ministry in your local body?

3. How can you further equip yourself to learn better ways of conducting your own personal ministry? Seek help from your pastors, if needed, to learn how you can be equipped.

For Groups:

1. Does your church emphasize each member's ministry in the body, or is it more of a "spectator" church where a few people conduct the ministry and the laymen are mostly spectators? If so, how could that be changed to make it be become more biblical?

2. Discuss what each member of your group thinks his particular ministry might be within the congregation.

3. What happens to a church when all of its members are properly active in the ministry of the church? What happens when that does not occur?

Meditation

Prayerfully think through the meaning and implications of Hebrews 3:12–13.

GREETERS
THE FIRST IMPRESSION

"Greet one another with a holy kiss. All the churches of
Christ send greetings" (Romans 16:16, see also vss. 1–15).
"Do not forget to entertain strangers, for by so doing, some
people have entertained angels without knowing it" (Hebrews 13:2).

In the Romans passage quoted above Paul passes along greetings
from the churches throughout the Roman Empire to the church at
Rome. Those words follow his personal greetings to twenty five individuals plus his greetings to the *church* which met at Priscilla's and
Aquila's home, to the *households* of both Aristobulus and Narcissus
and to the *brothers* who were associated with Asyncritus, Philegon,
Hermes, Patrobas and Hermas. These individuals and groups repre-
sent quite a large number of people. But the purpose for mentioning
this passage is to point out the personal attention that Paul gives to
these believers, and the affection that he has for them. Close personal bonds had been created between Paul and these people.

The Hebrews passage quoted above, while primarily addressing
the need to provide protection, fellowship, home and meal hospitality to strangers, implicitly enjoins the believers to greet people with
a willingness to help them. In order to properly exhibit hospitality,
believers must exhibit a loving, caring attitude to strangers. That is a
great need in the twenty–first century churches. Sadly, though, some
churches do not demonstrate that concern for those visitors who attend their services. Perhaps you have experienced the following:

You have visited a church at some time and come away saying,
"That was not a very friendly church." Not a single person came up
to you to speak to you. You had to locate someone yourself to ask
how to get to the morning classes and to even locate the sanctuary.
The music and the sermon were acceptable to you, but you were used
to a congregation that paid more attention to the guests. You felt
strongly that at least one person should have shaken your hand and

let you know that they were pleased that you were visiting. And so you left very disappointed and concluded that you would keep looking for another church.

When my wife was a young woman she had such an experience in a well-known church in our city. The pastor was a good expositor of Scripture and the music was theologically sound and uplifting. Because of those factors she attended the services for almost a year. But, during that entire year, *one* person spoke to her *one* time! No person ever called her, visited with her, came to her home, asked about her relationship with the Lord, or expressed any concern for her whatsoever. She could have been an unsaved person seeking the way of salvation, but no one would have known about it.

This church usually had an attendance of about 400 people. Certainly it was small enough that a person could not have gotten lost in the crowd. We were saddened to see a church where the truth was preached, but where there was an absence of any form of greeting or hospitality. We cannot help wondering what a lost person must have felt when he visited.

Contrast that experience with a visit the two of us made to a 12,000-member church in a large metropolitan area. When we arrived at their location we were immediately drawn to their information booth, where those attending were very friendly and helpful. The Sunday school class we attended had approximately 500 people. We were invited to sit around a large, round table with several other couples. The leader at that table immediately asked us about ourselves and then introduced us to the other people around the table and to the entire class as well. He, along with his wife, insisted that we come home to have Sunday lunch with them. We had a very enjoyable visit over the meal. As we were leaving they also invited us to the evening service and wanted to know if we could stay after the service for another meal with them. Our plans would not allow us to do so since we were only visiting the city and had other obligations. But we went away having made some new friends, we had information about the congregation and we felt both appreciated and loved. The Sunday School lesson was very good, as were the preaching and the worship. You can bet that if we had been planning to move to that city, we would have given that congregation serious consideration.

Each church must have some way to provide a sincere greeting to visitors. It is true that often the first impression is the lasting one. If your congregation, regardless of the size, has no such program, take it on yourself to help start one. Essentially all it takes is a smile, a handshake and asking the simple but genuine question, "May I help you?" As a matter of fact, you can do this yourself without any formal program. Here are some suggestions:

- Introduce yourself (and your family if they are available) to the visitor.

- Thank them for visiting and welcome them to your church.

- Get their names (and the names and ages of their children).

- Ask if they need the location of classes (and nursery, if needed).

- Give them a map of the church campus and a schedule of classes.

- Hand them a Sunday bulletin and any other visitor material available.

- Ask if there is any other information which they would like to have.

- If parking was a problem for them, explain where the visitors can easily park.

- Introduce them by name to their teachers and to others in the class.

- Make sure that they know how to locate the sanctuary.

- If possible introduce them to some members of the church staff.

- Invite them to any upcoming church activities.

- If possible, invite them to a Sunday meal.

- At some appropriate point try to determine their spiritual condition so you may either help them yourself or direct others to them.

- Encourage them to fill out the church visitor card.

The key point is that you want them to feel genuinely welcomed and assisted and that if they choose to return they will see you and others as people who have taken a personal interest in them. Great care should be taken to let visitors know that you are genuinely interested in them and not that you are just wanting to add another name to the church roll.

People will join a church (and stay with a church) because of relationships they have built with others in the body. Often they will return to a church they have visited because of that first encounter with the people they have met. Certainly the teaching, preaching, worship and other factors are critically important, but people will shy away from a congregation if they do not feel welcomed, or conclude that the church will present difficulties in forming relationships.

Application

For Individuals:

1. Does your church have official greeters?

2. If not, do you have laymen who serve in that capacity and if not, what about you offering to serve in that capacity? But keep in mind that you do not have to have an official title to serve. All members should assume this responsibility of extending a warm greeting to those who visit.

3. In your own church setting, what would be the most important functions that greeters could perform to help your church make visitors comfortable.

For Groups:

1. If your church does not have greeters, discuss how useful they would be and how you would go about getting those positions started.

2. In addition to greeters, what other positions in the church should be established which would help visitors feel more welcome to your church?

3. Does your church need to produce any brochures or pamphlets, or establish any other ministries in order to help reach new people and to help make those who come to feel more comfortable? Discuss.

Meditation

Prayerfully think through the meaning and implications of Romans 16:13.

CHAIRING A CHURCH COMMITTEE

"For God is not a God of disorder, but of peace" (1 Corinthians 14:33).

The context of these words from 1 Corinthians 14 is the matter of speaking in tongues. In the church some of the members were given the gift of tongues (in that context, foreign languages). Many of them were exercising that gift all at once, with no interpreters. There was mass confusion. And so Paul instructs them that they are to speak one at a time, no more than two or three per meeting and that there must be an interpreter to state what they were saying. Otherwise, people would have no idea what was going on and in the case of visitors, they would be totally confused. Paul reminds them that God is not a God of disorder ("confusion" in some translations).

We can have confusion in our churches today in different forms. This is especially true when trying to carry out the church's various ministries and attempting to meet the many needs which arise. For that reason, churches will often have a number of committees which help run the church activities. These will range from the Pulpit Committee, the Building Committee, the Youth Committee, the Long-range Planning Committee, the Finance Committee, the Women's Ministry Committee, to name but a few. Much time and energy are invested in these committees. And, sad to say, much of it can be wasted in these committee meetings. God wants us to be good stewards of our time and when it is squandered, God is not pleased. How, then, can we prevent time and energy spent on these committees from being useless?

If you are considering an offer to chair a committee, make certain that you have both the sufficient time to invest in it and the willingness to spend the appropriate time, skills, interest, energy and have the personality to make sure that it is run properly. If not, let someone else who does have those things chair the committee.

Here are some things which must be done to help a committee run smoothly (and will help prevent those meetings from becoming ones of disorder or confusion):

- Know clearly the purpose, scope and limitations of the committee.

- Choose as members of the committee people who are faithfully committed to the church and who can get along with each other.

- Regularly examine the purpose of the committee to see if it is really needed, or if it should be disbanded. Some committees are originally formed to deal with a specific problem but no longer serve a useful function. Yet, they continue to meet for years.

- Determine the proper size of the committee. Too few members can fail to provide sufficient input, or can put too much responsibility upon the few members. Too large a committee can become unmanageable.

- An agenda should be sent out well ahead of the meeting times. E-mail and faxes can be very useful to facilitate these notices.

- The chairman should always begin the meetings on time and end on time. Otherwise meetings can drag on for hours, wasting precious time.

- The chairman must keep the meetings on track with the agenda and know when and how to bring discussions back to the issues.

- The chairman must also have the insight and authority to appoint a sub-committee when that will expedite the committee's work.

- The chairman should have wisdom as to when a subject should be tabled for a later meeting.

- The chairman must not allow extraneous and unrelated subjects to become the focus of the meeting time.

- The chairman must be able to recognize when members' emotions are out of control and have the ability to restore order in the meetings.

- The chairman must be fair to all points of view and extremely careful that his bias does not prevent a fair hearing of all members.

- The chairman must make certain that no biblical principles are overlooked or violated and that the church constitution is followed.

- The committee must recognize that the church is under the rule of Jesus Christ and that He alone can make their work effective. Therefore, all the business conducted should be surrounded with prayer for wisdom and God's blessings upon any action taken.

- The committee may be called upon to take an action that will not be popular among the general membership. Therefore when possible, the committee chairman should provide relevant details to the membership to explain why that action was taken. Even then, there may be members who will disagree. The committee members must realize that one has to accept various risks (such as criticism or disagreement) when part of a decision-making body.

- Finally, often in committees, there are certain confidential matters which must be discussed. The chairman, members (and their spouses) must be able to keep things confidential until the appropriate time when they can be discussed openly. If prospective committee chairmen and members cannot be trusted in this area, they should not be put on the committee. It should also be pointed out that attempting to keep too many areas confidential could arouse unnecessary suspicion by the members. Therefore there must be a good and compelling reason to keep matters from the congregation.

Some churches elect to have no committees. The pastors, the elders, the deacons, or a combination of any of these operates such churches. There is no biblical rule in this area. Obviously, the Bible does sanction a pattern by which the elders are to serve as the chosen leadership. But beyond that, if the leadership should decide that various committees should be appointed, the church is violating no biblical passage in doing so.

Some argue that committees create a level of authority not sanctioned by the Bible and that a proliferation of committees creates an administrative burden for the church. In some cases that may be true. If the church leadership properly appoints them and if they are functioning properly, they may provide valuable advice to and support of the leadership. Each church has the God-given liberty to exercise its own prerogative in this area and to determine just how it shall operate. The leadership area is biblically prescribed, but how one goes about the administration of functions under that leadership is open for each church to determine for itself.

Application

For Individuals:

1. Are there areas in your church which need the attention of a committee? Discuss with your church leadership.

2. Think through the committees in your church and determine if your gifts could be used in those areas.

3. Are you qualified to be a committee chairman? Discuss that possibility with others and if they agree, consider offering to serve in such a capacity to the church leadership

For Groups:

1. Discuss the proper relationship which should exist between the various committees and the church leadership.

2. Are there committees in your church which have outlived their usefulness? Discuss among yourselves and if there is general agreement, bring these matters to the attention of the church leadership.

3. Think through the committees in your church and begin regu-
    larly praying for each committee as a whole and the members,
    individually, by name.

Meditation

Prayerfully think through the meaning and implications of
1 Peter 4:10.

YOUR HOME
A HOSPITALITY CENTER

"Be joyful in hope, patient in affliction, faithful in prayer. Share with God's people who are in need. Practice hospitality" (Romans 12:12–13).

All Christians would readily agree that we should be joyful in hope, patient in affliction, faithful in prayer and that we should share with those who are in need. When it comes to practicing hospitality, well that's a different story.

Paul does not make a distinction. He places us all under the same obligations. If we are to be joyful in hope, we are also to practice hospitality. If we are under obligation to share with those in need, then we are also to practice hospitality.

I have heard many describe hospitality as a special gift (based on 1 Peter 4:9) and by that definition, therefore, not an obligation for all believers. It seems that some believers do a better job of extending hospitality and therefore it is assumed that hospitality is one of their spiritual gifts. While Peter may be listing it as a special gift, Romans 12 commands it for all believers.

Perhaps the problem lies in the way we limit the concept of hospitality. We seem to define it by someone who has a spacious, accessible home and a bubbly personality. It is true that our Lord does bless certain people in those ways, but when you come back to Romans 12:12, all of us are obligated to extend hospitality. And in 1 Peter 4:9, every Christian is instructed to "offer hospitality to one another without grumbling."

Just what is hospitality? It can involve a number of factors. It is not tied to our having a spacious home or being in a certain economic level. It involves our attitude. Do we want to serve people? Are we willing to share whatever God has placed in our hands? Do we genuinely love people? Are we willing to be "inconvenienced" in order to meet the needs of others? Do we want other people to know that what is ours is really theirs also, because it ultimately belongs to God, and that we willingly and joyfully share it with them? Are we willing to see some of our possessions displaced or damaged for the good of others—both believers and unbelievers?

The command in the New Testament for believers to practice hospitality was often set in the context of opening one's home and heart to shelter other believers who were ostracized and persecuted by the pagan society in which they lived. Often they were driven from their families and homes and scattered, simply because of their belief in the risen Lord. It involved both inconvenience and great risk to offer hospitality to these persecuted fellow believers. In our culture, there is little or no risk (unless one lives in some of the Asian and Muslim countries, where Christians are subject to great persecution even today). For most of us, hospitality is simply a matter of a small inconvenience.

Because we often associate hospitality with our homes, here are some ways in which we can use those homes for the good of others. We can offer our homes for:

- Home Bible Studies

- Home Cell Groups

- A place for traveling evangelists or conference speakers

- A place for visiting missionaries

- Sunday School parties

- Hosting singles' groups

- Hosting youth activities

- Hosting dinners for the staff or pastors

- Providing dinners for international students

- Hosting Christian singing groups who may be traveling in our area

- A temporary place to stay for those families who move into our area

- Hosting dinners for the senior members of the church (golden agers)

- A place for various church committees to meet

- A place where children can be provided for when their mothers need a day out

- By taking in people who do not have a home

This list could be endless. Each church situation will have a different set of needs. Perhaps such a list could be developed and posted just to give members an idea of how and when they could serve in this area.

Even more important than our house is our attitude. Others need to know that we are genuinely pleased to offer for their use whatever God has blessed us with, and that we count it a joy to serve in this capacity. And they need to know and feel that they are important to us, not that we are offering our time, energy, home and possessions in a merely perfunctory manner.

There are some inherent "liabilities" when one begins to practice hospitality. For example:

- Our homes will suffer more wear and tear.

- Our carpets may suffer spills and may wear out more quickly.

- There may be more marks on our walls.

- Our furniture may be broken or scratched more often.

- Our lawns may suffer some abuse.

- Our phone line may get tied up.

- We may even find an occasional unknown long distance charge on our bill.

- We may help others who seem to show absolutely no gratitude.

- We may get physically worn out serving others.

- Their schedules may interrupt some things we had planned.

- We may realize that we are being called on to help in this manner much more than others who could do just as much as we do.

- Often for those traveling through our area we may have to drive them to their obligations and back and forth to the airport or bus station.

No doubt our wives will catch the bulk of the work. They probably could add many other things to the above list. The point here is that practicing hospitality in our culture can be work. It can also be very rewarding. Some of our very best family friends are those with whom we have shared our home or property, or who have shared their possessions with us. The love and warmth felt in both directions have been a positive reinforcement of the bond that we share together as believers.

Sharing with unbelievers can be a bit more trying on us, but our godly example can be a powerful witness to them. When our lives are being lived as Christ instructs us, they can see a clear difference between the world they are used to and a world that they never knew existed. And when we reinforce that with a respectful, patient, clear, verbal presentation of the gospel, it will often fall on more receptive ears.

James tells us that not many of us should be teachers because we will be judged more strictly. Not all have the gift of leadership. Not all are equipped to serve as Deacons. But Paul calls on all of us to practice hospitality. Obviously the size of our homes, the price of our homes, the quality of our furniture, the location of our homes, plus a host of other matters will all be different—and often irrelevant.

Some will be able to host a large number of people, while others may have a small apartment where only a few people can physically gather. But if the desire is there, there will be some way in which our home can be a hospitality center. It may be only to invite a new visitor to our home for a brief visit, or a sandwich and a coke, or a place to spend the night. Our attitude is what will be most important. In the matter of hospitality, it is true that "if there is a will, there is a way" to share what God has placed into our custody.

Application

For Individuals:

1. Recognize that nothing you "own" is really yours. God has simply placed you as a custodian over those possessions for a period of time. God wants you to use His property for the good of His kingdom (Matthew 25:14–30).

2. Acts 16:15 and 16:40 tell us that after her conversion Lydia offered her home. For what two purposes?

3. Assess your home situation. What size function could you host, either inside or outside?

4. What groups are you personally drawn to—Youth? Golden Agers? Visitors? Home Cell Groups? Others?

5. Plan to personally invite others to your home. Also contact your church leaders and let them know that your home, your automobile, your property are available for certain functions.

6. Pray that God will make you joyful for the opportunity to serve Him in this capacity—even when there may be spills on your new carpet!

For Groups:

1. Cite examples where you have seen hospitality bring benefits to your local church.

2. What can your group do to practice hospitality to others?

3. Discuss specific ways in which Christians can practice hospitality to other Christians, to strangers and to the lost within your community.

4. What happens within a church when this command of hospitality is not obeyed?

Meditation

Prayerfully think through the meaning and implications of Matthew 25:34–46.

PREPARING FOR
A LEADERSHIP ROLE

"The reason I left you in Crete was that you might straighten out what was left unfinished and appoint elders in every town, as I directed you" (Titus 1:5).

In this passage the apostle Paul is giving Titus instructions to appoint (or ordain) church leadership in all of the towns on the island of Crete in which a church is meeting. The instruction is followed by a listing of the qualifications for an elder (vss. 6–9; see also 1 Timothy 3:1–7 and 1 Peter 5:11–4). Apparently Paul has not had sufficient time to finish the job of selecting or appointing church leadership. Knowing the need of leadership in each church, Paul is now asking Titus to complete the task.

There has been a great deal of material written about the biblical method of selecting or appointing church leadership. Some argue that they should be selected by existing church leaders. Others would argue that they should be chosen by the church membership. And there are some denominations in which church leaders are chosen or approved by the collective voice of leaders who serve in some manner over the churches in that denomination (such as a presbytery). Regardless of the method of installing church leadership, it is obvious that there must be people selected who will lead the church.

In the New Testament, apart from apostles, prophets and evangelists, two offices are named: Elder (pastor, overseer, bishop, minister) and Deacon. The Elders are to be the spiritual leaders of the body and the Deacons are chosen to attend to the physical and financial needs of the body. This does not rule out committees being appointed to serve under these two offices and leadership within these committees. For example, a church could have a Building Committee, a Pastoral Search Committee, a Nursery Committee, or a Financial Stewardship Committee. All such committees should report to the Elders and/or Deacons.

Whether one serves as an Elder, a Deacon, or a Committee Chairman (or member) or in some other leadership role, there need to be some basic qualifications and possibly some training. In our congregation, we have both a Pastoral Training Center (in which seminary level courses are offered along with eleven course hours of practical training) and also an Elder Training Program where potential elders are taught and trained. While these are two separate programs, often a man will be involved in both at the same time. In addition to the book learning, he is also being trained on a very practical level in the work of an Elder.

Some churches have a "Junior" Elder and Deacon program in which the potential Elders and Deacons meet with the group and are assigned specific projects to test and improve their skills and qualifications for the job. Without voting privileges, these men are beginning to serve on a very practical level without being given the official status or title of a church leader. Those who meet the qualifications are then elevated to one of those offices.

In addition to programs set up in the various churches, the church should be on the lookout for men who exhibit potential leadership qualifications. When those men are spotted, they should be encouraged to begin preparing themselves for a leadership role. They should be directed in ways to improve their Bible knowledge, how to build a personal Bible study library, how to minister among the flock, how to lead, perhaps encouraging them to take public speaking courses, to read good literature on leadership within the church, to attend seminars or conferences in which good, practical advice is given and to locate ways to improve themselves in any area in which they exhibit a need.

There are two excellent books on the office of Elder and Deacon written by Alexander Strauch: *Biblical Eldership: An Urgent Call to Restore Biblical Church Leadership* and *The New Testament Deacon*, both published by Lewis and Roth, Littleton, Colorado. Candidates for these two offices would be tremendously helped by the material offered in these two works.

In far too many churches there is only one leader, the pastor. If that is by design, it is not biblical. In all of the New Testament passages which speak of church leadership, it always speaks of a plurality of leadership. God's wisdom can be seen in establishing a plurality of leadership, for two or more heads are generally much better than one. There is wisdom in many counselors (Proverbs 12:15; 13:10; 15:22). Also, being the one leader is often a very lonely task. Because decisions made are often questioned, and the one leader can find it very frustrating to have no one else to whom he can turn in those situations. When there is multiple leadership in a church, varying points of view can be expressed and this can often lead to more accurate analysis and better plans. Each church should be constantly on the lookout for men who can be trained to step into a leadership role in order to provide a continuous flow of qualified leaders.

You have undoubtedly noticed that all of my discussion has been centered around men. That has been purposeful because in the New Testament God has ordained that men must be the leaders in both the church and the home (1 Corinthians 14:33b–38; 1 Timothy 2:8–15). However, women play a very important part in the success of any church. They may serve in a myriad of activities, even serving in a leadership role among the women. The only thing which they cannot do is to serve as a leader or teacher over men. In everything else they are permitted and encouraged to serve. Without their excellent service, most churches would be in a sad state of affairs. We men must continually thank God for the wonderful way in which He has women serving in our churches. For further information on the many areas of service in which a woman is permitted to serve, see the article in Section Seven, "Just What Can a Woman Do in the Church?" (p. 239–244).

Application

For Individuals:

1. Are there leadership areas within your church in which you would consider serving? If so, make that known to the existing leadership and ask in what training you should be involved to prepare yourself for such service.

2. What areas of need in your church do you think would thrive if there were a committed leader who would take charge of those areas?

3. Do you regularly pray for your church leaders? List areas in which you need to remind yourself to pray for the leadership within your church body.

For Groups:

1. What does the New Testament teach regarding multiple church leadership? Does your church practice multiple leadership?

2. Discuss areas of your church which need strong leadership. What are you praying for God to do in these areas? What can you do to help meet this need?

3. What happens to a church when the leadership is weak or ineffective?

Meditation

Prayerfully think through the meaning and implications of Philippians 1:1.

Section Six

Problems in the Body

UNITY AND DIVERSITY

"This mystery is that through the gospel the Gentiles are heirs together with Israel, members together of one body and share together the promises of Christ Jesus" (Ephesians 3:6).

Paul speaks of God's mystery and manifold wisdom (Ephesians 3:10) when he speaks of the New Testament church. The mystery was that both Jews and Gentiles would be brought together harmoniously in the same household of God.

That almost seemed like an impossibility. The early Christians had to be taught over and over again that this was God's plan (Acts 10, 15, Ephesians 3, etc.) These two races of people were vastly different in almost every respect. To bring them together to worship in the same body took nothing less than the grace of God. Yet, God brought unity in the midst of such diversity. In fact, that was an important part of the New Testament message.

As I think of the church in which I am presently a member, I see great diversity. There are people of many backgrounds, different colors of skin, varying educational levels, wide varieties of occupations and financial resources, singles, young families and older couples, coming from many states and even different countries. Yet God has woven a beautiful unity into our fabric despite such a wide diversity.

It has often been said that in no other place could such a large group of people with such an amazing diversity regularly come together around a central theme and agree! Yet, that is the way God intended His church to be. And when you think about it, such diversity has great benefits for the body. Consider the following:

- Diversity helps open our eyes to people who are different from us.

- Diversity brings different and, often, healthy ways to assess matters.

- Diversity brings together gifts to the body of which the congregation might otherwise be deprived.

- Diversity enables those with an abundance of means to help those members who are without.

- Diversity brings those who are capable of leadership together with those who need leading.

- Diversity brings those who have spiritual foresight alongside those who are more task oriented. Both are needed.

A church needs all types of members in order to be a well-rounded community.

Amid this great diversity, God desires unity. In fact, it is one of His often-repeated commands (e.g. Philippians 1:27–2:16; 4:2–3). Because we struggle with a sinful nature, such differences can create difficulties. Often we feel comfortable only when things are done our way. That's our comfort zone—the way we have always done it! Certain people will share our perspectives and we will naturally gravitate to them. But God wants us to work harmoniously and to love the *entire* body. And so He often directs us toward unity.

Our unity is to be "in Him." It is not uniformity (such as we see in some cults). "Unity in Him" means that though we may come from different perspectives, we must recognize that our ultimate purpose is to preach Christ and to build up the body. To do this in peace we must consider other members more important than ourselves. Our particular ideas, methods and feelings should be placed below those of others in the body unless, of course, there is a clear biblical principle at stake. Ultimately, the good of the entire body must be our goal, not the particular point of view we hold.

What we have just said is particularly difficult, but Christ has shown us the way. It was not for His personal pleasure that He came to be deprived, made the object of scorn and derision, to suffer, bleed and die the death of a criminal, then to be buried in another man's grave. Yet He put aside His personal interests for you and me. He considered us more important than Himself, even more important than fellowship with His father (Philippians 2:6-11). And though we were totally unlike Him, yet He brought us together by making peace by His blood shed on the cross (Colossians 1:20).

By His sacrifice He has brought together millions upon hundreds of millions, from across this globe, from generations and generations of people, from all walks of life and tremendously varying backgrounds, to be unified into the one Body of Christ, that great congregation which someday will be presented to the Father, without spot or blemish (Ephesians 5:27). That is a picture of great unity amid tremendous diversity. Our responsibility in our local body is to follow the perfect example of our Lord in helping to create and maintain deep unity within an amazing amount of diversity.

Application

For Individuals:

1. Are you comfortable among other Christians in your congregation who are different in many respects from you?

2. Are there factions in your church simply because people have different backgrounds?

3. If there are any problems because of these differences, what can you do to help your congregation become more unified?

4. Are there some non-negotiables which you must stand by even though they may create some disunity? What are some of them?

For Groups:

1. Discuss the differences between the biblical concept of unity and that of uniformity.

2. What are some ways in which your church needs more unity?

3. What happens to a church when it is seriously lacking in unity?

4. What can members of your group do to help create more unity within your church body?

Meditation

Prayerfully think through the meaning and implications of James 2:1–9.

CHURCH PROBLEMS
BE PART OF THE SOLUTION

"I plead with Euodia and I plead with Syntyche to agree with each other in the Lord. Yes and I ask you, loyal yokefellow, help these women who have contended at my side in the cause of the gospel… "(Philippians 4:2,3a).

A church is a group of called out people who commit themselves together to minister to each other, to worship together and to individually and collectively penetrate the lost world around them and across the globe. It would be ideal if all of the members were genuine Christians who never allowed a sinful problem to arise to create a disruption within the body. But until the Lord returns, we will never live in an ideal world, nor serve in an ideal church. There has never been and will never be a perfect church on this earth. True, some churches are more problem-free than others, yet because of our sinful natures, problems arise. When they do, what is our responsibility as members?

First, we need to determine if the issue is a matter with which members should be concerned. Or, should we bring it to the attention of leadership and let them deal with it? For example, if it becomes apparent that the youth pastor is lazy and not doing his job, or the contributions seem to be disappearing, or there is a Sunday School teacher who is teaching something unbiblical, the leadership of the church must be informed. If the leadership is adequately investigating the matter and conscientiously working on it, then we should let them bring the matter to a conclusion. It can only create harm for us to second-guess these men along the way. We need to quietly pray for their wisdom and courage. We do not need to talk to others about these problems. If other members bring these issues to our attention, we need to encourage them to simply pray for the leadership as they handle these matters. If there are public issues, which need public disclosure, then we should let the leaders determine when and how that should occur.

But what about those situations where the leadership will not become involved and you fear that things will get much worse? If it is a matter of serious sin or an issue that will seriously harm the welfare of the body, we have a responsibility to address the matter. Even then we should inform the leadership of our intent. At every level, care must be taken to adhere to all biblical standards. The good of the entire body must be kept in mind.

Now, what about more private matters? Suppose you know that two brothers in the church are in the middle of some dispute. You think that you are capable of getting the two of them together where you could serve as an arbiter. You could begin by discussing the matter separately with each brother and then collectively with them both. It would probably be wise to seek counsel and to have additional spiritual witnesses to help insure that all of the steps covered by Matthew 18:15-17 are obeyed.

What about those matters where there is no apparent sin, but where things are simply not working well? Perhaps you and others think that the preaching pastor does not have the gift of preaching and that the membership is declining because of it. Or, the Sunday night children's program is just not working out, or the Wednesday family meals are being attended by fewer and fewer people and it appears that given enough time the dinners will simply die out. Many of the members are talking about these problems, but none seem to be doing anything about them. They are creating more and more dissatisfaction and people are beginning to show serious signs of moving to other congregations because of these matters.

Again, these issues should be respectfully brought to the attention of the leadership and if eventually nothing is done, as a member you should try to help to improve the situation, if that is feasible. Get involved in the solution! Pray for the Lord's enabling grace toward those involved in these ministries—that God would increase their knowledge of the situation, give them wisdom and improve their skills in their area of service. Pray for and urge others who are critical to be patient encouragers.

The point of this discussion is to remind us that as members, we have the responsibility to bring solutions to problems that may occur in the body. Yet, we have biblical ways to address them. We cannot idly sit by and assume that problems will go away. Often they will only get worse. We may not be a part of the problem, but can and should definitely be part of the solution. Our responsibility is to know the proper channels to follow, and to offer help toward solutions in the proper spirit.

Application

For Individuals:

1. Think about any serious problem in your congregation of which you are personally aware.

2. Are you presently encouraging biblical solutions to this problem?

3. What, specifically, can you be doing to help solve this problem?

For Groups:

1. Is there a problem in your congregation which you as a group should be helping to solve?

2. Cite hypothetical examples of problems in a church about which you should only pray, and those in which you should become personally involved.

3. When church problems occur, is that a sign of a weak church? Or could it be that the way those problems are solved demonstrates the health of a church?

4. Give unspecified examples of church problems that were incorrectly handled, and others that were handled biblically.

Meditation

Prayerfully think through the meaning and implications of Romans 14:19.

OUR CHURCH IS WEAK

"Yet I hold this against you: You have forsaken your first love… If you do not repent, I will come to you and remove your lampstand from its place" (Revelation 2:4–5).

There are weak churches. There are sick churches. There are dying churches. There are dead churches!

That's biblical truth. Of all of the local churches mentioned in the New Testament, few, if any, have remained to this day. Most, if not all, eventually died. Sounds very depressing, does it not? If it were not for the universal church which never dies, the prospects for our work in Christ's kingdom would seem rather futile. Given enough time, our church may eventually die. And yet every member must continuously devote himself to the vibrancy of his own local congregation.

What should we do when our church is weak? First, we must make an honest assessment to determine its malady. Is it poor leadership; unbiblical preaching; too small a body to have multiple ministries; members who are lethargic, unloving, full of tension, selfish, not evangelistic? Unless we know the problem with which we are dealing, we surely cannot help correct the problem. And we must make certain that our analysis is based on biblical principles rather than some worldly standard of performance.

Second, we need to know how to correct the deficiencies. This is where we need to know the proper biblical solutions. Human methods, apart from Scriptural guidelines, can only make matters worse. For example, to help build up the membership by adding chili suppers and bingo games will probably only create a congregation of lost people. Instead, perhaps a series of home Bible studies will help us truly reach people for Christ.

Third, we need to commit ourselves to bringing biblical solutions to the church. We must adopt the position that it is not the other person's responsibility, but our own. We must also realize that we may have to go it alone, that others may not see the need as we do.

Here is a very general and brief set of steps we may follow when we recognize that our church has become weak:

- Work through established leadership.

- Pray for specific needs in the congregation.

- Encourage others both by your example and through your speech.

- Persevere in all the things which you set your hands to do.

- Do your part and more than your part.

- Allow an appropriate time for changes to take place.

- There may come a time when we have done all we can and must recognize that the matter seems hopeless. For the good of our spiritual lives and that of our family, we may be forced to choose another congregation (but only after we have exhausted all of the biblical remedies).

Some churches are in such a weakened condition that restoration seems an impossibility, but we must never give up easily. It is amazing what God can do when there is just a small flicker of life remaining. Our sovereign Lord has many surprising ways of transforming and re-energizing local congregations.

Application

For Individuals:

1. What evidence do you have that your church is alive?

2. Is there evidence that your church is weakening?

3. What can you personally do to help restore your church?

For Groups:

1. What are the elements of a weak church? A dead church? A strong church?

2. What should be your role in trying to strengthen your own church?

3. If you were to see signs that your church is dying, what should you do?

Meditation

Prayerfully think through the meaning and implications of Revelation 3:1–3, 14–22.

SHOULD I CONFRONT
MY FELLOW MEMBER?

"Brothers, if a man is trapped in some sin, you who are spiritual should restore him gently. But watch yourself; you also may be tempted" (Galatians 6:1).

The Bible clearly instructs us that if our brother sins we are to confront him. Does it not also teach forbearance toward others (Ephesians 4:2; Colossians 3:13)? What about judging someone else? Doesn't it teach us not to judge others (Matthew 7:1)? And what about Galatians 6:1–5, where it instructs us that we are to share one another's sin burden? Just how do we put all of these seemingly contradictory instructions together properly and then live them out appropriately? Here are some thoughts.

We must clearly distinguish between what is sin and what is a matter of preference. If the Bible does not declare something as sin, either directly or by implication, then we have no right to approach a brother simply because we disagree with something he has done, or the way he has done it, except perhaps, to lovingly help him learn a better way.

This is an extremely important principle. Many people have been seriously offended or turned off by other individuals who self-righteously condemn them on the basis of personal preference. When one begins to substitute his own personal preferences in place of the objective standard of the Word of God, serious problems can occur.

Our love for the brother should make us quick to forbear when there are less serious sins, especially when they are non-recurring. Suppose a brother becomes momentarily angry, or on the spur of the moment demonstrates some selfishness. Neither is a pattern of his life. These are matters about which we should forbear (bear up under), unless and until we see a pattern develop. And when we see a pattern developing our appeal to him should spring from both humility and patience. No doubt we, too, have sinful patterns in our lives and must never approach our brother harshly or with a spirit of pride. In fact, we should always approach our brother assuming that he will want to do the right thing.

In Matthew 18:15–17 we are instructed as to how to go to our brother who sins and will not repent. The steps are laid out clearly as to private confrontation, then taking witnesses, then exposing the matter to the church and then ultimately carrying out the solemn step of excluding the erring brother from our fellowship (see the section on "Church Discipline: A Biblical Responsibility" p. 107–111).

This command by Christ in Matthew 18 is clearly addressed to each church member. We cannot wait for the next person, or the church leaders, to begin the process. When our brother clearly sins and shows no sign of repentance, we are to approach him. In cases where there is a willful sin or deviation from the truth and when the brother is not willing to resolve the matter, the steps as outlined by Christ in this passage are to be observed.

To what type of sins is Jesus referring which would lead us to eventually exclude a non-repentant brother? Looking at some other portions of Scripture can be very instructive at this point. Though this is not an exhaustive list, here are some of the critical areas:

- Divisiveness (2 Thessalonians 311; Titus 3:10–11; Romans 16:17–20).

- Unruly, disorderly and undisciplined living (2 Thessalonians 3:6, 11, 14; 1 Thessalonians 5:14).

- Conflict between members (1 Corinthians 6:5; Philippians 4:2–3).

- Sexual impurity (1 Corinthians 5 and 6).

- Denial of the great doctrines of our faith or advocating heretical teachings (1 Timothy 6:3,5; 2 Timothy 2:16–18; Titus 3:10; 2 John 1:10–11; Revelation 2:14).

The above passages talk about those who are idle busybodies, who cause divisions, are contentious, are sexually immoral, those who are greedy, idolators, slanderers, drunkards, swindlers, false teachers, liars, and those who have wandered away from the truth.

A proper heart attitude in discerning and dealing with our erring brothers is clearly called for in the Word of God:

- We are to avoid vengeance and arrogance while humbly praying for God's guidance (Galatians 6:1).

- We are to view the individual as an erring brother and not a bitter enemy (2 Thessalonians 3:15).

- We are to approach him with sorrow and not with harsh criticism (1 Corinthians 5:2; 2 Corinthians 2:4).

- We are to maintain a forgiving spirit and be ready to extend forgiveness and reconciliation as soon as repentance occurs (2 Corinthians 2:7; 7:10–11).

Confrontation of a brother and eventual church discipline has as its objective to recover the brother to a position of obedience, to protect the integrity of the name of Christ, to purify the church, to deter sin in the congregation and to reconcile the brother to the body.

No doubt many will ask, "Did not Jesus instruct us in Matthew 7:1: "Do not judge"? How can we reconcile that command with the above New Testament requirements? The way we do so is to understand what Jesus was really saying. It is clear from the Scriptures that we are to judge teachers, we are to judge sins and we are even to judge ourselves (1 Corinthians 11:31). In fact, Christ and His apostles made judgments on many, many occasions. Here the use of the term judge or judgment is used with the sense of thinking properly and making correct judgments (or proper conclusions).

The key to understanding what Christ said in Matthew 7:1 is to keep reading through verse 5. And what we find is that Christ is talking about a censorious judgment where we are attempting to self-righteously condemn others for their sins as though we had never sinned. Christ tells us to first deal with our own sins and after having done that, then we shall be in a position to look into the sins of others. In fact, in verse 5 Christ tells us that after we have removed the log from our own eye, then we shall be able to clearly see the speck in our brother's eye. That implies that we still have an obligation to help our brother overcome his sin. Self-righteous, censorious judgment is what Christ is condemning; not lovingly, patiently judging our brother who has sinned and then doing whatever we can, with the proper spirit, to restore him to obedience.

We have a clear biblical obligation to confront our brother. But what we choose to confront him over and the way we go about it can make all the difference in the world. It can drive him away, make a spectacle to the world, cause much disruption and can involve ourselves in sins of our own. Or it can demonstrate to all concerned that Christian principles work when applied biblically.

Application

For Individuals:

1. Is there a member in your congregation whom you should confront?

2. Though you will never be perfect in this life, is your Christian walk such that you can conscientiously approach another member?

3. Give an unspecified example where this has been done inappropriately. Give an example where it has been done properly and successfully.

For Groups:

1. Give hypothetical examples of things that are committed by fellow members, which you should confront. Give examples of those things that one should forebear.

2. What should be the steps and your attitude when you confront a brother?

3. How can you know when you are judging another person biblically and when you are doing it improperly?

4. What are the ultimate goals hoped for when a brother is properly confronted over a matter?

Meditation

Prayerfully think through the meaning and implications of Galatians 6:1–5.

OUR TONGUES CAN HELP
DESTROY A GOOD CHURCH

"With the tongue we praise our Lord and Father and with it we curse men, who have been made in God's likeness. Out of the same mouth come praise and cursing. My brothers, this should not be" (James 3:9–10).

That non-bony, flappable instrument between our bicuspids can be an instrument of tremendous good or cataclysmic destruction. It can be used to build people up in the faith or to destroy their hard-earned reputations. It can help bring about peace among nations or can start a war. And it can be an instrument for good in a local church, or can destroy a work of God.

Not only does James recognize the importance of our tongues and address their awesome purposes, but Proverbs is also replete with advice about our tongues: Proverbs 2:6; 4:24; 5:1–4; 6:12; 8:6–9; 10:11, 13, 14, 18–21, 31, 32; 11:9, 11–13; 12:6, 13, 14, 18, 25: 13:2, 3; 14:3, 23; 15:1, 2, 4, 7, 23, 26, 28; 16:1, 10, 13, 21, 23, 24, 27, 28; 17:4, 7, 9, 20, 27, 28; 18:4, 6–8, 13, 20, 21; 20:15, 19; 21:23; 22:11, 12, 17, 18; 23:15, 16: 24:1, 2, 26, 28; 25:9–15, 23; 26:4, 5, 17–18; 27:2; 28:23; 29:5, 20; 30:10; 31:26.

As a Christian and in the church, it is essential that we carefully use and guard our tongues. Some of the most common misuses of our tongues are:

- Gossiping about fellow members.

- Criticizing the sermon.

- Running the pastor down.

- Passing along matters which should be kept confidential.

- Constantly questioning the leadership's methods and motives.

- Setting two members against each other.

- Talking about dirty and immoral issues.

- Making subtle, negative references about others.

- Talking of matters about which we are uninformed.

- Making disparaging remarks to others.

- Bragging about our accomplishments and acts of service.

- Encouraging church disharmony.

Clearly, these uses of our tongues are wrong and can do great damage in a church. James reminds us that our tongue is like a small spark which can ignite a fire leading to tremendous destruction (James 3:5–6).

Yet, we can take each one of these situations, turn them around and use our tongues for good. Let's do that:

- If a fellow member has a problem, go to him and try to help be part of the solution. Don't go to someone else to talk about the matter.

- If the sermon is lacking, ask for a private audience with your pastor and lovingly help him see where his message could improve.

- If there is something in your pastor's lifestyle that seriously detracts from his effectiveness, privately point this out to him and help him improve.

- When confidential matters are brought to your attention, constructively remind the person that in the future, for the good of all parties, the matters should not be discussed with anyone else.

- Ask for a private audience with the leadership to express your concerns. In many cases your perception of wrong may be because you are lacking full information. Once satisfied, use your tongue to pledge your support and prayers.

- Always be about the work of establishing and maintaining unity. Use your tongue to teach love, unity, forgiveness and patience.

- Never pass along something immoral. Quote Ephesians 5:3–7 to the person who brings you such information or stories. Pray with them that God will teach us all to remain clean in our wicked world.

- Whatever is honorable and lovely about people should be our topic of discussion—not subtle, destructive references.

- Ask for information so you will be fully informed. Never speak on any issues unless and until you are sure your information is correct.

- Our conversation is to be seasoned with salt—and for upbuilding. Disparaging remarks hurt and destroy and only drive wedges between us and our brothers and sisters, for whom Christ gave His life.

- Realize that God is the One who bestows gifts and brings about successes. Talk about the good deeds of others as a way to encourage the body.

- Use your tongue to help settle church squabbles. Often refer others to such passages as Proverbs 16:27–28 and Philippians 2:1–16.

As church members, we can make a difference between a church that brings glory to Christ and one which becomes a spectacle to the world. Proverbs 10:11 reminds us that "the mouth of the righteous is a fountain of life."

Application

For Individuals:

1. During the past week has your tongue been used in a destructive manner?

2. If so, ask the Lord right now to forgive you and to help you correct your sin.

3. Make a list of ways in which you want to improve the use of your tongue.

For Groups:

1. Look up, read and discuss a number of the passages given above which talk about our tongues.

2. Cite examples to the group in which your own tongue has done harm.

3. Cite examples where you have seen the tongue active in doing great good.

4. What is it that causes us to misuse our tongues?

5. What are some ways for us to improve the control of our tongues?

Meditation

Prayerfully think through the meaning and implications of Ephesians 4:29–32.

WHEN AND HOW
TO LEAVE A CHURCH

"I know your deeds, that you are neither cold nor hot. I wish you were either one or the other! So, because you are luke-warm—neither hot nor cold—I am about to spit you out of my mouth" (Revelation 3:15–16).

Seven local churches were addressed in Revelation, chapters 2 and 3 and of the seven, six of them were severely chastised by our Lord. And it seems that the strongest words were reserved for the last church, Laodicea. Our Lord says that they are "wretched, pitiful, poor, blind and naked" (vs. 17) and that He is so sick of their luke-warmness that He is ready to vomit them out of his mouth!

None of the seven churches exist today. That is very sad, but also very instructive. A church is but a generation away from apostasy. Churches do go astray. Churches that for a period of time are a bastion of truth and a haven for the lost can become theologically and practically corrupt. And when that occurs, a true believer cannot continue to support that body. Leaving that church becomes a re-sponsibility.

Yet, that is not the reason why most people leave their churches in our generation. I have both heard of and witnessed people leaving churches for a host of other reasons, such as:

- Because they disagreed with the pastor

- Because they disagreed with a member

- Because they disagreed with an Elder or Deacon decision

- Because the church practiced church discipline

- Because the church did *not* practice church discipline

- Because the church moved to a new location

- Because the sermons were too long

- Because the sermons were too short

- Because of disagreement with the doctrinal statement

- Because the church was "too liberal"

- Because the church was "too strict or legalistic"

- Because the church did not have a youth program

- Because the youth program did not meet with their approval

- Because they did not like the children's or nursery programs

- Because the preacher was no longer preaching the truth

- Because the preacher was boring

- Because of the pastor's personal political views

- Because the church down the street was more exciting

- Because the music program included choruses

- Because the music program did *not* include choruses

- Because the music program used only the song books

- Because the music program did *not* use the song books

- Because the church did not have a Sunday School program

- Because the church did not have a regular Sunday night service

- Because of the way the church handled the money

- Because the church supported some wrong causes

- Because the member was not asked to serve in the church

- Because the member was asked to do too much in the church

- Because the member had to work too often in the nursery

- Because someone was teaching who should not have been

- Because that member or another member was not allowed to teach

- Because they wanted the church to go into a building program

- Because they did *not* want the church to go into a building program

- Because a certain pastor was called to the church

- Because a certain pastor was *not* called to the church

- Because of the church's views on eschatology

- Because of the church's views on smoking, dancing, alcoholic beverages, or movies

- Because the church had a kitchen and people ate at the church

- Because they were not chosen as a church leader

- Because they were not a "good fit" in that church

- Because of the way people dressed in that church

- Because the people were unfriendly in the church

- Because of something someone said to them in the church

- Because the people in that church were above their social class

- Because people in that church would not accept them

- Because they could not find real fellowship in that church

- Because most of the people in the church were too old

- Because most of the people in the church were too young

- Because the church leadership would not listen to them

- Because the preacher "preached too often on money"

- Because the church was "just going in the wrong direction"

- Because "nobody ever noticed me"

- Because the pastor "did not even know my name"

- Because "I never heard from the pastor"

- Because "when I was sick, nobody came to see me."

- Because "when I missed church, nobody even noticed or called me"

- Because "my family will be happy in another church"

- Because "my children don't want to come to that church anymore"

- Because "my children aren't getting anything out of the sermons"

- Because "the church just asks too much of me"

- Because "there are just so many things I am unhappy about, I don't want to even talk about them"

- Because "I just want to visit around"

Perhaps you have recognized some of these reasons—and even used some of them yourself. I do not mean to depreciate all of them because some of the reasons given above do have some validity. My point here is not to evaluate each of these reasons, but rather to discuss in general how such matters should be approached, before one does leave a church. Departing a church is a serious matter and one which usually affects not only the family who leaves, but also those who are left behind, especially the church leadership. Someone has described it as something like a family breaking up (the church is a family). There can be much heartache to many people when people leave a church.

There are legitimate *reasons* for leaving a church. And there are legitimate *ways* to leave a church. Just walking away with no explanation or no attempt to right any wrongs is not the proper way. Yet, it is the way many people leave.

Here are some things which must be done before one leaves a church:

- We must check our motives very carefully.

- Our reasons must be well grounded and clearly articulated.

- We must be in regular, earnest prayer about the matter.

- We must guard our tongues very carefully.

- We must be extremely careful that we do not unnecessarily create unrest in other members.

- Our discussions with the leadership must be characterized by love.

- Our attempts to correct matters must be with great respect, care and patience.

- If our concern is over personal preferences, rather than biblical matters, we must consider others' interest more important than ours.

- Great care should be taken that we submit to the leadership of the church, unless we determine with proper counsel that there is a serious biblical issue at stake.

- If the leadership will listen, we need to give them plenty of time to consider the matter.

- If the leadership will not listen to us, or will not take proper action to correct the matter and we are thoroughly convinced that there is a serious biblical issue, we should ask for a meeting of the church in which to express our concerns.

- We should ask ourselves what we have personally done to correct any wrong or deficiency in the church with which we are concerned.

- We should evaluate if our leaving would do harm to an otherwise good church.

- We should never leave, nor encourage others to leave, unless we are thoroughly convinced that one or both of the following conditions exist: (1) that the church has become an apostate church (where serious unbiblical teaching or practices are allowed), or (2) that we are convinced that, over the long haul, we cannot find a place to serve in the church, or that our families will not be spiritually fed in that body.

I am convinced that if these suggestions were given careful attention, there would be fewer people leaving churches. In our culture people flip around from church to church in almost the same way they change from one automobile to another, always looking for something a bit more new and pleasurable. That is not the essence of Christianity.

Christ called on us to serve one another, not to be seeking our own comfort. He certainly gave us the supreme example. The welfare of others is why He came to this earth, suffered abuse and extreme discomfort and, ultimately, the horrible death of a vile criminal on the cross of Calvary. He could have moved from this earth and taken up a comfortable residence in heaven, rather than having to suffer at the hands of sinful men. Yet He set His sights on the good of others, rather than those of His own, and gave His all. That is how much He loved the church.

Christ's example often demonstrates how cheap our view of the local church can be. We ask how the church can serve us, rather than how *we can serve Christ* through His local bodies. He exhibits extreme patience with us; how can we do otherwise for His people, for whom He died?

The next time you think about leaving a church, think of the example of Christ. He does not just walk away from His people, but patiently suffers with them through many trials and tribulations, always thinking of their needs before His own. While He did warn the seven churches in Revelation and eventually took away their right to exist, He did so only after patiently urging them to repent. He gave them an opportunity to change. We can do no less!

Application

For Individuals:

1. Is there an area in your church which you think needs correction?

2. Are these biblical matters or matters of personal preference?

3. Have you properly approached your church leadership about them?

4. What should you, personally, be doing about these matters?

For Groups:

1. What are some of the reasons you have heard for people leaving a church?

2. For what biblical reasons should a person leave a church?

3. Before people leave a church, what steps should they take?

4. If leaving a church, what attitudes should they express and what should they look for in a new church?

5. Is it ever right to leave a church? Is it biblical to quit going to church for a period of time "to just take some time out?"

Meditation

Prayerfully think through the meaning and implications of Galatians 6:9–10.

Section Seven

Miscellaneous

INTERPRETING GOD'S WORD

"Your word is a lamp to my feet and a light for my path...
Your statutes are wonderful, therefore I obey them. The un-
folding of your words gives light; it gives understanding to
the simple. I open my mouth and pant, longing for your
commands" (Psalm 119:105, 129–130).

Properly knowing and obeying God's Word is of paramount importance to the believer. His Word is a light for our path and without it we grope in the darkness. Misunderstanding and misapplying
God's Word has brought about many heresies and ungodly practices.
Therefore, to properly interpret God's Word is a key ingredient to
the believer's growth in holiness and his protection from heretical
influences which would invade his soul.

To *interpret* is to "clarify the meaning of; elucidate; to expound
the significance of... to offer an explanation." *Hermeneutics* is "the
science and methodology of interpretation, especially of Scriptural texts." It is tempting to discuss the large field of hermeneutics.
However, that would be a book in itself and so we will be content
to list some of the very broad, general ideas of proper biblical interpretation. [1]

Two other terms need a simple definition. *Exegesis* is "to draw
the meaning out of a text." That is the *proper* way to interpret Scripture. It lets the text itself tell what it is saying. *Eisegesis* is "to read a
meaning into a text." That is an *incorrect* way to interpret Scripture.
Rather than letting the text itself tell what it is saying, in eisegesis
one brings his own meaning to the text.

---

[1] Most of the material in this section has been gleaned from some notes
prepared by a friend, Bill Simmons, but adapted and modified for use here and
used by permission. These are somewhat standard principles of interpretation (or
hermeneutics). Though many books on interpretation could be cited, I suggest
the following one, because it is written in non-technical language and should be
very easy for the layman to follow: J. Scott Duvall and J. Daniel Hays, *Grasping
God's Word—A Hands-On Approach to Reading, Interpreting and Applying The Bible*
(Grand Rapids:, MI: Zondervan, 2001).

Here are three very broad, vital steps to take in biblical interpretation:

1. *Observation.* In this step one should read, think, look for, ask questions (such as who, when, why, where, how), investigate, etc.

2. *Interpretation.* Here one applies all of the hermeneutic principles to understand what the writer actually meant in his context, generation and society.

3. *Application.* In this final step the reader should attempt to learn what the proper interpretation leads us to think, to feel, to do, to be involved with.

When beginning with *observation* here are some suggestions to follow:

1. Read the passage:

   - Devotionally

   - Repeatedly

   - Inquisitively

2. Ask the questions:

   - *Who?* Who wrote or spoke these words? About whom is the passage talking? To whom are these words addressed?

   - *What?* What kind of literature is this? Poetry? Narrative? Direct teaching? Prophecy? What is the atmosphere of this passage? Calm? Emotionally intense? Fearful? Rejoicing? What happens in this passage? What precedes this passage and what follows it? What do I learn about God, Jesus Christ, the Holy Spirit or mankind in this passage? What is God doing in this passage? What difficult words are here and what do they mean? What will happen if I follow this person's example? What will happen if I obey the command God gives here? What will happen if I later ignore what I'm learning in this passage?

- *Where?* Where does the action in this passage take place?

- *When?* When did the action occur?

- *Why?* Why did the speaker or writer communicate these words? Why did God allow this to happen? Why did certain people respond as they did? Why did Jesus say what He said?

- *How?* How should this passage affect my life? How would I have handled the situation presented in this passage? How did God work in someone's life in this passage? How does this passage relate to other parts of Scripture?

3. Look for the following:

   - Find key words—strong, emphatic words; action verbs; repeated words.

   - Identify cause/effect statements—"if...then."

   - Underscore commands—calls for action.

   - Examine linking words—"and, but, because, as, since, when, for, therefore, after."

4. Find out the thrust of the passage:

   - What is the central thought—the big idea?

   - What are the corollary or supporting ideas?

5. Mark the passage:

   - Box key words, repeated words.

   - Circle linking (connecting) verbs.

   - Parenthesize modifying phrases.

   - Color, underline positive or negative sins, truths, etc.

6. Outline the passage:

   - Write down the basic unit of thought.

- Under that head, jot down the progression of thought.

Now that *observation* of the passage is completed, the next step is *interpretation*. At this point do the following:

1. Bridge the language gap:

    By using good, multiple translations and competent original language word studies.

2. Bridge the cultural gap:

    By using Bible introductions, Bible dictionaries, Bible encyclopedias, to learn what the culture was like at the time of the writing of that portion of Scripture.

3. Bridge the geographical gap:

    By learning from some of the above sources the geography of the biblical setting.

4. Bridge the historical gap:

    By learning just what was going on at that point in history, with the Israelites, the early Christians and those nations and kingdoms around them.

5. Cross reference:

    Refer to other portions of Scripture where the names, events, ideas, words, are presented.

6. Follow the literal principle:

    Unless there is legitimate reason for not taking the words literally, such as metaphors, allegories, personifications, take the words literally.

7. Follow the grammatical principle:

    Pay attention to verbs, nouns, pronouns, prepositions and conjunctions.

8. Recognize figures of speech:

    Determine if this is a metaphor, simile, personification, hyperbole, irony, allegory or proverb.

9. Interpret in light of the entire teaching of the Bible:

    If your interpretation is in conflict with the clear teaching
    of the remainder of the Bible, you have not interpreted
    properly.

10. Use the proper text:

    There are some variant readings, as is often indicated by
    footnotes. Attempt to ascertain the most reliable text.

11. Understand the context:

    This is probably the most important step in proper bib-
    lical interpretation. Attempt to understand the overall
    context of the Bible, the context of the book which you
    are studying, the context of the section of the book you
    are in and the immediate context of the particular passage
    you are interpreting.

12. The use of common sense:

    While this can be misused, it is a reasonably reliable
    safeguard. If it just doesn't make sense, your conclusions
    should be checked and re-checked.

Once we have followed the principles of our *observation* and *interpretation*, we have now come to the third step, that of *application*.
If we stop at the second step and do not apply the truths and principles to our lives, we have read and studied the Bible in a manner
which God never intended. He does not want us to simply know
what the Bible says, He wants us to obey what it says. He wants us to
internalize it into our own lives. And so when we come to the point
of *application*, we must ask ourselves questions such as:

1. What new way does God want me to think?

2. What thoughts does God want me to give up?

3. What new way does God want me to feel?

4. What feelings does God want me to give up?

5. What does God now want me to do?

6. What does God want me to quit doing?

7. What is it with which God wants me to be involved?

8. What is it with which God does not want me involved?

This completes the cycle: *Observation, Interpretation* and *Application*. Many times these steps are overlooked, or the order is reversed and Christians attempt to apply Scripture without having properly interpreted Scripture. When doing so, unbiblical practices can result, creating havoc within the church.

When the Scriptures are properly interpreted and applied, they become, in the words of the Psalmist (quoted above), "a light for my path … wonderful … giving understanding to the simple."

There is one last point which needs mentioning. We can follow all of these principles very carefully, but unless the Holy Spirit removes the scales from our eyes, we will still not properly interpret and apply God's Word. As you open God's Word, realize that it is "His" Word and only He can make it plain. Ask Him to do so for you!

Application

For Individuals:

1. Do you need to purchase some basic tools to help you interpret Scripture?

2. Using the above principles, take a small portion of God's Word and attempt to interpret and apply it.

3. Consider forming a group of believers (perhaps even with some unbelievers—as a possible means to witness to them) and begin collectively studying God's Word in the manner prescribed above.

4. Purchase and read the book, *Grasping God's Word*, mentioned in the footnote above.

For Groups:

1. Cite examples of unbiblical principles of interpretation and, as a result, where Scriptures have been misunderstood.

2. Choose a passage of Scripture and collectively attempt to properly interpret it using the above principles. Perhaps the leader of the group could choose the passage beforehand so the group members could be working on it before meeting together.

3. Cite several examples in which it is imperative that one understand the context in order to properly know what the Scriptures are actually conveying.

4. Give examples where you have seen *eisegesis* committed, rather than *exegesis*.

Meditation

Prayerfully think through the meaning and implications of Matthew 7:24–27.

JUST WHAT CAN A WOMAN DO IN THE CHURCH?

"As in all the congregations of the saints, women should remain silent in the churches. They are not allowed to speak, but must be in submission, as the Law says. If they want to inquire about something, they should ask their own husbands at home; for it is disgraceful for a woman to speak in the church" (1 Corinthians 14:33b–35). "A woman should learn in quietness and full submission. I do not permit a woman to teach or to have authority over a man; she must be silent" (1 Timothy 2:11–12).

Of the many instructions in the New Testament with regard to the church, these verses have been the occasion of some of the most heated controversy. Some have taken them so literally as to prevent a woman from uttering a word of any type in the church, even to ask a question. Others have relegated these verses to mere custom in the first century and think they have no instructive value to the modern church. Some women in the church react strongly to these verses, while others are happy that God has called men, rather than women, to lead the body.

To keep the discussion here as simple as possible, I want to emphasize only two things.[1] First, I want to state clearly what the verses say a woman may not do within the church and second, I want to provide a list of some of the many, many other ways in which women *may use their gifts* to serve our Lord.

---

[1] To enter into a discussion of all of the various views and to build the support for the position which I think is correct, would require too much space. However, here are some very good sources which will amply explain and defend the proper role for women, both in the church and in the home: Wayne A. Mack and David Swavely, *Life in the Father's House—A Member's Guide to the Local Church*, Ch. 5, "Fulfilling our Roles as Men and Women," (Cherry Hill, NJ: Mack Publishing, 1972), 71–92; and *The Role of Women in the Church* (Phillipsburg, NJ: Presbyterian

The verses say that there are only two things which a woman *may not do*: (1) A woman may not teach a man; and (2) She may not have authority over a man within the church. Both of these prohibitions are in the *context of the local church*. These verses say nothing about their activities in the home, in a school, in a neighborhood, at work, or anywhere else.[2] In both of these passages Paul is telling us that men are to be the recognized leaders of the body. Men demonstrate that leadership by their teaching and by exercising authority over the body.

Peter adds an important point that must always be remembered by leaders: they are to serve as examples to the congregation and are not to lord it over the flock in a dictatorial manner (1 Peter 5:1–4). Such loving, sacrificial leadership makes submission much easier, especially for the women in the church when they know that the leaders are there to protect them, to care for them, to feed them and to pray for them.

It is impossible to list all of the ways in which women are biblically permitted to serve our Lord. But here are just a few ways in which women are permitted (and encouraged!) to be engaged, within both the local and the universal church.

Women may:

- Teach other women and children in the church (probably over seventy-five percent of the membership), teaching them in Sunday School, VBS, Awana, Bible studies, etc.

- Disciple or mentor other women.

---

and Reformed, 1996); Anne Ortland, *Disciplines of the Beautiful Woman* (Waco, TX: Word Books, 1977); Martha Peace, *Becoming a Titus 2 Woman* (Bemidji, MN: Focus Publishing, 1997); and *The Excellent Wife* (Bemidji, MN: Focus Publishing, n.d.); Barbara Hughes, *Disciplines of a Godly Woman* (Wheaton, IL: Crossway Books, 2001); John Piper and Wayne Grudem, *Recovering Biblical Manhood and Womanhood* (Wheaton, IL: Crossway Books, 1991).

[2] With regard to the home, it is clear that the man is to be the head of his household (see Ephesians 5:21–33). In carrying out his headship in the home he is to love his wife in the same way that Christ loved the church, giving His life for her. It is to be a sacrificial, giving love. When a husband loves his wife in this manner, submission is easy for the wife.

- Disciple or mentor teenage girls.

- Practice stewardship.

- Serve on mission teams.

- Assist in planting churches.

- Help raise godly children.

- Counsel women and girls.

- Sing and play musical instruments.

- Write letters of encouragement.

- Work in pro-life and adoption ministries.

- Teach in a Christian school.

- Work on Christian radio programs.

- Comfort those men and women who grieve and suffer.

- Work in singles' ministries with girls and women.

- Visit elderly men and women and help them with their needs.

- Provide various help to women in need—new moms, over-worked ladies, discouraged people, widows, divorcees.

- Assist care-givers.

- Open their home to others and to church activities.

- Share with those in need.

- Contribute financially to the church and its ministries.

- Offer to baby sit, clean, run copies, answer phones, prepare teaching materials or crafts.

- Organize people for needed projects.

- Design curriculum.

- Create and maintain a database for the church membership, Sunday School program, a church class, children's groups, a Bible study.

- Coordinate a drive to collect needed items in order to promote sharing within the congregation.

- Write letters to Congress or other governmental leaders about spiritual issues.

- Teach elderly ladies in assisted-living facilities.

- Prepare and deliver devotionals to women and children.

- Interview Christians and write their stories or testimonies.

- Write or arrange hymns, poems and Christian music.

- Use creative skills to benefit others.

- Do evangelistic work in women's prisons.

- Teach in a mission school.

- Conduct conferences for women.

- Coordinate travel for short-term missions groups.

- Teach English or computers, or other needed courses in a foreign (closed) country where informal evangelism can be done.

- Teach pastors' wives in undeveloped countries.

- Counsel single teen mothers, pre-abortion or post-abortion women, women in problem marriages, abused women, unhappy singles, mothers of difficult or rebellious children, lonely divorced or abandoned women, women with addictions, women in sinful relationships, women facing serious illness or death, overwhelmed and depressed women.

- Visit orphans and widows.

- Assist those caring for aged and ill parents.

- Direct or assist in women's ministries, children's ministries, team counseling of women and families.

- Work in children's events and clubs, music ministry, Christian education, youth ministry, financial planning and administration, small group ministries, mission coordination and communication, church communication.

- Organize and be involved in various prayer groups.

- Serve as church secretary or financial secretary.

- Serve as the church librarian.

- Operate information booths at church.

- Serve on hospitality teams.

- Be a part of a community evangelistic team.

- Serve on the benevolence committee.

- Offer your services to the crew that cleans, decorates, or repairs the church building.

- Prepare the church bulletin.

- Develop and distribute the church prayer list.

- Answer phones for the church and direct calls.

- Make hospital visits.

- Operate the church food pantry for the poor.

- Serve as the church photographer.

- Operate the church tape ministry.

- Publish, write, illustrate, or edit Christian books, magazines, newspaper columns and articles.

This list could be almost endless. The point here is that though women are not permitted to teach or to have authority over men, there are ample opportunities for them to be at work in the body of Christ. In fact, as the above list demonstrates, there is more work for them to do than they will ever have time for. Their service in these many areas is very much needed, is meaningful and is of eternal significance.

Churches should, therefore, encourage women to find their areas of service and to serve there with all of their hearts.

Application

For Individuals:

1. Are there women in your church leading or teaching in areas where the Bible forbids?

2. What other areas in your church exist (other than those listed above) where women should be serving?

3. Have you thanked God for the tremendous work being performed by the women of your church?

For Groups:

1. What are some of the most important contributions that are being made by the women of your congregation?

2. Beginning at what age would you specify that children should be taught by men—junior high, senior high, college?

3. What do you think about women leading men in a job, profession, armed services, or other organizations? Is the Bible explicit in these areas?

Meditation

Prayerfully think through the implications of the faithful services of the many women mentioned in Romans 16.

MISCELLANEOUS QUESTIONS, PROBLEMS AND CONCERNS

"Whatever you do, work at it with all your heart, as working for the Lord, not from men, since you know that you will receive an inheritance from the Lord as a reward. It is the Lord Christ you are serving" (Colossians 3:23–24).

The strength of this command becomes clearer when we realize the context in which it was given. Slaves were being commanded to obey their masters. There was probably nothing more difficult than serving as a slave to another human being, especially if that master was "harsh" (literally, "crooked, bent, morally crooked, perverse, the opposite of good," 1 Peter 2:18). And yet Paul (and Peter would also agree) reminds the slaves that they are to work in that situation with all of their hearts, as working for the Lord. That situation required genuine faith!

Now, when we transfer that concept to our service in the church, how much easier it should be for us to accept our church responsibilities with joy! And yet, as easy as we have it, sometimes we don't want to put ourselves out in the area of service. So, here are some quick questions, problems and concerns and some short answers. I hope these very brief answers will help jar us into right thinking.

Should I be involved in a Para-Church Ministry?

Answer: The church is the pillar and foundation of the truth (1 Timothy 3:15). In the church is where you should primarily serve. But there may be para-church ministries which are meeting needs which the church has not been able to meet. If you can participate biblically and if your involvement does not take away from your responsibilities at your church, go ahead and serve. But always seek to turn those helped by a para-church ministry toward a sound local body. That's doing business God's way!

What is acceptable worship?

Answer: Primarily, obedience—in any area! That is what God wants. The form will vary from church to church, from society to society and from generation to generation. Obey God and He will accept your worship.

Surely there are better teachers than I am!

Answer: There probably are. But perhaps for reasons unknown to you, they are not teaching. Let others—especially the church leadership—help you assess your qualifications. If God has given you a gift in that area, He wants you to use it.

Our church is not friendly.

Answer: What are you doing about it? Make a list of how you can help in this area. Then set about to systematically make a difference!

I cannot stay awake in church.

Answer: Maybe it is because you are staying out, or staying up too late, on Saturday nights. Change or get control of your schedule so that you can get some rest and be prepared to join in worship on Sunday. If your medication is making you drowsy, talk to your doctor about it to see if he can make a change for you. Or he may spot another medical problem that is causing your drowsiness. Pray for those involved in the service and encourage them when they do well. Take notes during the sermon—outlining the presentation. Summarize the points and the major Scriptures used. This often helps. If all of these fail, perhaps you should examine yourself about your interest in spiritual matters.

Should our church go in debt with a building program?

Answer: That's too loaded a question to answer here. But it is a question which the entire church should answer very carefully. It probably would be wise also to bring in a professional church financial counselor to help assess the church's needs and ability. Don't allow the church to be overloaded with unneeded debt. That may disrupt the fellowship of the church and rob the church of her ability to meet other more pressing needs. It is not wrong for a church to be in debt, but the amount of debt could be wrong. But keep in mind that God may be leading your church to sacrifice heavily for a new, larger facility for a new generation which He is planning to reach with the gospel.

What can I do? I am disabled and must stay at home most of the time.

Answer: Can you write notes and letters of encouragement to the church staff and members? If you can't afford the postage, ask the church to help you with it. Do you have a telephone? Call people, visit with them giving words of encouragement and praise to God. Ask the staff for the names of some lonely people and develop a telephone ministry to them. Or ask the church staff if you could help them with something at home. Don't sit there doing nothing, wasting whatever gifts and the time God has given you.

I have been betrayed or disappointed by other believers—some in our own church.

Answer: You are not alone. Many believers have been hurt by other believers. Even Christ was betrayed by His own apostles and is betrayed by us daily. That's the nature of the fall and our inherent depravity. Forgive or forbear, depending upon the matter. But don't let it fester in your mind. Just remember that you've probably hurt others in ways which you did not recognize and you've been forgiven.

My children want to attend another church.

Answer: Is your church preaching Christ and biblical truth, ministering to the members, reaching out to the lost, reaching out to the entire family—even the children? If not, do what you can to remedy that with encouragement to those now ministering. If the church is not a good church, maybe the entire family should move its membership. But do not let your children make the family's decisions. Adults are to lead the family, not children!

You mean I need to cut the church's grass?

Answer: Are you physically able and will your work schedule allow it? YES, you may need to serve your church in that manner. If not, maybe you could help pay someone to cut the grass at church. You do need to be serving others.

I've got my own teenagers; I don't need to help raise some more at church.

Answer: If you are really needed to serve in the youth area, why not? If God has gifted you to serve there, then use that gift. And, after all, aren't others at the church trying to help your children grow spiritually? Probably some of the youth workers don't even have teenagers of their own, yet they are serving you and your children! You do need to be serving others.

You mean that I need to work in the nursery and the children's ministry?

Answer: Yes, unless you have mental, physical, or moral problems which would keep you from doing so. Why should others have to carry your share of the load? If you are already carrying a sufficient number of other responsibilities in the church, perhaps you should be excused. But if not, is there a good reason why you should be excused? You do need to be serving others.

When I was sick, nobody came to see me.

Answer: Did you or your family let others know that you were sick? Use your telephone. Let your pastors and fellow members know that you need someone. Swallow your pride; reach out to others. Then if nobody comes, or expresses concern, your church does have a problem and you can be a part of the solution when you get well.

I can't afford to dress the way they do at church.

Answer: God is not offended by the way you dress, unless it is immodest or in unusual ways that draw attention to yourself. Wear what you have and what you can afford. God sees what is inside. Please Him, not others.

Please don't ask me. I have enough kitchen duties at home.

Answer: Can you cook, wash dishes, sweep the floor? Then do it when you are needed and don't complain. Count it a privilege to serve Christ in any way. Men, we are not exempt either!

When is "turning the cheek" suffering abuse?

Answer: Seldom! But it can occur. You'll surely know when it occurs, but if not, give a Christian friend and/or the church leadership the full details and let them help you decide.

I know of a businessman who professes to be a Christian, but who does not operate his business that way.

Answer: There are probably many of them! But have you personally talked with the man? If he is a member of your church have you followed the proper steps of church discipline? God has ordained the way to deal with sin; follow His prescription. It makes no difference whether the man is a businessman, a professional athlete, a teacher, or an artist. Sin is sin and God has told us how to deal with it. But first, see if you have a log in your own eye!

What can I do at the church office?

Answer: What are you skills? Computer work, answering the phone, making copies, ordering supplies, cleaning the office, filing, doing the library work, making tapes and mailing out bulletins or tapes are possibilities. Call the church and give them the days and times you can work. If for some reason they cannot, or prefer not to use you, accept their decision and ask them to help you find a need that you can meet. They will find a place for you!

What can a teenager do?

Answer: Listen, learn, pray, encourage others, witness to the lost around you, offer to serve anywhere you are needed, keep yourself morally pure, study the Word, be obedient to your parents and kind to your siblings, do your home chores happily and thank God regularly that He loves teenagers!

I'm very shy and I haven't had much success in one-on-one witnessing.

Answer: God is the One who ultimately gives success to our witness. Don't give up, keep trying. But in the meantime maybe you can give out Bibles, or good books, tracts, or tape recordings. Or maybe you could write letters to people in which you appeal to them to turn to Christ. There are many ways to witness. Your life is your most effective witness, but people must hear (or read) the gospel. You can get it to them in ways other than your own voice. To whom should you give or send these things? Your family, your friends, your neighbors, your co-workers, your classmates, the repair people who come to your home, your paper boy, the one who cuts your lawn, the man who takes care of your automobile. There is a vast field out there. Every person is going down one of two routes: either heaven or hell. Do what you can to get them on the right road!

How much should we pay our pastors?

Answer: As much as we can! Those who are working hard at the ministry deserve double honor (1 Timothy 5:17). Don't be stingy with them. Make their service a joy for them, for that is to your profit (Hebrews 13:17). Don't muzzle the ox when he is treading out the grain (1 Timothy 5:18). At least let him live the way the average person in the congregation does, not exorbitantly, nor meagerly, but fairly. Don't make him have to worry all the time about meeting the expenses with the lifestyle you expect of him. His mind should be on the ministry to the sheep.

My pastor has not called me in a year!

Answer: Have you called him? Give him a call and say, "Hey, I need to hear from you." He will respond then, you can bet, and if he is unintentionally ignoring others, that might call his attention to it.

The Lord has taken my spouse and I am so lonely!

Answer: Do you desire to remarry? If so, make yourself available, but not too quickly. Listen to the advice of your family and friends. In the meantime, get more involved in the service to the church.

Don't sit around feeling sorry for yourself. As a single person you should have more time to serve the Lord. Work is good therapy, especially if you are doing something of eternal significance. And anything done for Christ and His people is eternally significant!

I don't like that person at church. How can I love him?

Answer: We, ourselves, were Christ's enemies by nature; how could He have liked us? Yet He loved us (Romans 5:10). Love is not an emotion (though it does affect our emotions). Love (*agape* love) is seeking the person's highest good, which is what Christ did for us. Christ turned us, His enemies, into His friends. Maybe through agape love you can turn that person into a friend.

It is so hard to forgive, especially when I have been deeply hurt.

Answer: That is true, because we are sinners! By nature we want justice and revenge and we want to nurse that hurt for a long time. It is quite simple, though. If we cannot forgive (upon true repentance), Christ makes it clear that we will not be forgiven (Matthew 18:35). If we have been forgiven a debt of $10,000,000 how can we *not* forgive our brother who owes us a mere $20 (Matthew 18:21–25). We deserve hell, yet we get heaven—all because Christ forgives us. Meditating on that ought to make us want to forgive others!

CONCLUSION
Dying to Self

"It is true that some preach Christ out of envy and rivalry, but others out of good will. The latter do so in love, knowing that I am put here for the defense of the gospel. The former preach Christ out of selfish ambition, not sincerely, supposing that they can stir up trouble for me while I am in chains. But what does it matter? The important thing is that in every way, whether from false motives or true, Christ is preached. And because of this I rejoice" (Philippians 1:15–18a).

In this passage the great apostle Paul is in chains for Christ in a Roman prison. While there he is reaping a spiritual harvest as many souls are being saved by his verbal testimony and his joyful attitude despite his incarceration. Yet, within the Roman church there are those who are jealous of Paul's success in the proclamation of the gospel. They are trying to stir up trouble for Paul. In the middle of that situation, Paul is rejoicing because Christ is being preached—by these same people. His emphasis is not that they are giving him trouble—but rather that Christ is preached!

That is a prime example of "dying to self."

In the Christian church, service often requires a dying to one's self. At times when we render service there will be misunderstanding, unjust criticism and deep heartache. These are hard to endure. Yet, we are called upon to serve as Paul did, but more importantly, as our Lord did, who sacrificed everything for the good of others. Christ willingly abandoned His glory in heaven with the Father, His comfort, His reputation, His very life (Philippians 2:6–8). He truly died to self!

As we serve in our local church body, may God give us grace to follow the example of our Lord by our using everything that God has put within us to serve others.

This book closes with the words of another who died to self by signing this poem "anonymous"—rather than taking credit for his work:

When you are forgotten or neglected or purposely set at Naught, and you sting and hurt with the insult of oversight but your heart is happy, being counted worthy to suffer for Christ—that is dying to self.

When your good is evil spoken of, when your wishes are crossed, your advise disregarded, your opinions ridiculed and you refuse to let anger rise in your heart, or even defend yourself, but take it all in patient loving silence—that is dying to self.

When you lovingly and patiently bear any disorder, any irregularity, or any annoyance, when you can stand face to face with waste, folly, extravagence, spiritual insensibility, and endure it as Jesus endured it— that is dying to self.

When you are content with any food, any offering, any raiment, any climate, any society, any attitude, any interruption by the will of God—that is dying to self.

When you never care to refer to yourself in conversation, or to record your own good works, or itch after commendation, when you can truly love to be unknown— that is dying to self.

When you see your brother prosper and have his needs met and can honestly rejoice with him in spirit and feel no envy nor question God, while your own needs are far greater and in desperate circumstances—that is dying to self.

When you can receive correction and reproof from one of less stature than yourself, can humbly submit inwardly as well as outwardly, finding no rebellion or resentment rising up within your heart—that is dying to self.

When we can willingly and joyfully die to self while serving in the context of our local church, then we have truly learned what it means to be *living in the Body of Christ*.

RESOURCES

This is a very selective bibliography dealing with the church, its ministries and our responsibilities. There are many excellent works covering these areas and it was tempting to include many of them. However, the following books have been included because of their biblical content, their easy-to-read style and their choice of material covered. To have included an exhaustive bibliography might have been discouraging to you, the reader, who may not have the time and money to delve so deeply into such a study. So I have chosen to limit the list to these book.

The Church:

Getz, Gene. *Sharpening the Focus of the Church*. Chicago, IL: Moody, 1974.

MacArthur, John. *The Body Dynamic*. Colorado Springs, CO: Chariot/Victor, 1996.

MacArthur, John. *The Master's Plan for the Church*. Chicago, IL: Moody, 1991.

Mack, Wayne A. and David Swavely. *Life in the Father's House— A Member's Guide to the Local Church*. Phillipsburg, NJ: Presbyterian and Reformed, 1996.

Maoz, Baruch, Hulse, Eric and others. *Local Church Practice*. Haywards Heath Sussex, England: Carey Publications, 1978.

The Church's Leadership:

Adams, Jay E. *Shepherding God's Flock*. Grand Rapids, MI: Zondervan, 1974.

Ascol, Thomas K., ed. *Dear Timothy: Letters on Pastoral Ministry*. Cape Coral, FL: Founders Press, 2004.

Eyres, Lawrence R. *The Elders of the Church*. Phillipsburg, NJ: P & R Publishing, 1975.

Sanders, Oswald. *Spiritual Leadership*. Chicago, IL: Moody, 1967.

Strauch, Alexander. *Biblical Eldership: An Urgent Call to Restore Biblical Church Leadership*. Littleton, CO: Lewis and Roth, 1988.

Strauch, Alexander. *The New Testament Deacon*. Littleton, CO: Lewis and Roth, 1992.

Thomas, Curtis C. *Practical Wisdom for Pastors*. Wheaton, IL: Crossway Books, 2001.

The Church's Work:

Adams, Jay E. *Competent to Counsel*. Grand Rapids, MI: Zondervan, 1970.

Adams, Jay E. *Handbook to Church Discipline*. Grand Rapids, MI: Zondervan, 1986.

Adams, Jay E. *Ready to Restore*. Phillipsburg, NJ: Presbyterian & Reformed, 1982.

Getz, Gene. *Building up One Another*. Wheaton, IL: Victor, 1986.

Keller, Timothy J. *Ministries of Mercy*. Phillipsburg, NJ: P & R Publishers, 1997.

Mack, Wayne A. *The Role of Women in the Church*. Cherry Hill, NJ: Mack Publishing, 1972.

McRae, William. *Dynamics of Spiritual Gifts*. Grand Rapids, MI: Zondervan, 1976.

Whitney, Donald W. *Spiritual Disciplines Within the Church*. Chicago, IL: Moody, 1996.

Wright, Eric. *Church—No Spectator Sport.* Durham, England: Evangelical Press, 1994.

The Church's Divine Manual (The Bible)

Fee, Gordon D. and Douglas Stuart. *How to Read the Bible for All It's Worth.* Grand Rapids, MI: Zondervan, 1981.

Fee, Gordon D. and Douglas Stuart. *How to Read the Bible Book by Book.* Grand Rapids, MI: Zondervan, 2002.

Wilkinson, Bruce and Kenneth Boa. *Talk Thru The Old Testament.* Nashville, TN: Thomas Nelson, 1983.

Wilkinson, Bruce and Kenneth Boa. *Talk Thru The New Testament.* Nashville, TN: Thomas Nelson, 1983.

MacArthur, John. *How to Get the Most from God's Word.* Dallas, TX: Word, 1997.

McDowell, Joshua. *Guide to Understanding Your Bible.* San Bernardino, CA: Here's Life, 1982.

The Church's Outreach

Aldrich, Joseph C. *Life-Style Evangelism: Crossing Traditional Boundaries to Reach the Unbelieving World.* Sisters, OR: Multnomah, 1981.

Little, Paul E. *How to Give Away Your Faith.* Downers Grove, IL: InterVarsity, 1966.

Metzger, Will. *Tell the Truth: The Whole Gospel to the Whole Person by Whole People.* Downer's Grove, IL: Inter-Varsity, 1981.

Piper, John. *Let the Nations Be Glad: The Supremacy of God in Missions.* Grand Rapids, MI: Baker, 2003.

Printed in the United States
68271LVS00003B/85